Partition
Through My Eyes

Partition
Through My Eyes

Kishanlal Budhiraja

ALLIED PUBLISHERS PVT. LTD.

Noida • Mumbai • Kolkata • Chennai • Bangalore

ALLIED PUBLISHERS PRIVATE LIMITED

D-5, Sector-2, **Noida**–201 301
Ph. Nos.: 0120-4320295/2542557/4352866
E-mail: delhi.books@alliedpublishers.com

17 Chittaranjan Avenue, **Kolkata**–700072
Ph.: 033-22129618 • E-mail: cal.books@alliedpublishers.com

15 J.N. Heredia Marg, Ballard Estate, **Mumbai**–400001
Ph.: 022-42126969 • E-mail: mumbai.books@alliedpublishers.com

No. 25/10, Commander-in-Chief Road, Ethiraj Lane (Next to Post Office)
Egmore, **Chennai**–600008
Ph.: 044-28223938 • E-mail: chennai.books@alliedpublishers.com

P.B. No. 9932, No. 15, 3rd Floor (Next to Vijaya Bank), 5th Cross, Gandhinagar, Karnataka, **Bangalore**–560009. Ph.: 080-41530285/22386239
E-mail: bngl.books@alliedpublishers.com

Website: www.alliedpublishers.com

ISBN: 978-93-48699-79-4

Edited by Dr. Nishtha Anilkumar

Cover page design and illustrations by Ms Shilpi Dey

Published by Sunil Sachdev and printed by Ravi Sachdev
at Allied Publishers Pvt. Ltd., D-5, Sector-2, Noida–201 301

Preface

This is the story of our father from August 1947 to April 1948 (he was eleven years old) as remembered by him for many years and finally penned down by him in 2012 (when he was 76 years) after a lot of prodding from us (son and daughter). He passed away in September 2012.

This story not only brings the partition alive but also tells us something about survival in adverse conditions, the social fabric of a Punjabi family and the education system then. I would have loved it if he had narrated the stories of a few latter years too – from 1948 to 1960 till he moved to Delhi. I have tried to keep the flow of his writing as it is to give the flavor of how vividly he remembered those days even after 60 years.

The partition, even though traumatic, did not dampen his positive spirit ! He studied till SSLC and took up a job to support the family. Understanding the importance of education, he did his graduation in 1969–70 when we were very young. He retired as a Depot Manager in Pfizer Ltd in 1996. I remember he could create Urdu couplets in a jiffy in any small social get together! He remained a stock market and sports enthusiast till the end. Education being the only investment for him, he encouraged both of us to pursue higher studies always.

15 August, 2025

Dr. Nishtha Anilkumar and
Mr. Kismet Budhiraja

Contents

Independence

You turn the pages of history. You will notice every era has been full of upheavals. At the root of all such upheavals has been – power crazy individuals. Our era is no exception. In the present day era we are the victims. A few individuals were over ambitious and had unyielding ego.

These attributes were well exploited by the British rulers of our country. They had succeeded in using their policy: Divide and Rule. Some of our top brass leaders fell into their trap. The result was division of our country in to two parts: Hindustan and Pakistan.

It might have satisfied the lust of power of some power crazy individuals. But the country paid a very heavy price. Lakhs of people suffered: loss of life, loss of material wealth and loss of the legacy inheritance of their ancestors. We the legacy inheritors continue to suffer unnoticed. More importantly the deep rooted generations were up-rooted never to flourish there again.

It was 12th August, yes, I distinctly recall 12.08.1947. In the 2nd last period our Maulvi Saheb (Head Master) sent a note reading as "*Agar aap ke waldain, parson – 14.08.1947 ko school aane se manna karen to bhi sab ko school aana hai*" (In case your parents do not allow you to come to school, tell them that it is mandatory for you to go to school on that day and you are going to school).

Ours was a primary school up to 4th class. It was the only school for 11 villages. It was a boys school. There were no school uniforms. We were advised to wear white shirt and white salwar on that day – 14.8.1947.

Those days the girls were not allowed to attend the school. Thus there was no school for girls. In case parents wanted that their daughter should learn how to read and write, she was taught at home in the local language. My eldest sister Bhiranvan Devi learnt *Gurumukhi* at home from our *bhua* – aunt. She was initiated to recite *Guru Granth Sahib* at *Gurudwara*, the place of worship near our house. Our village was village of Hindus. The temple was out of the village surrounded by big and tall shady trees. In the afternoon many men would take their cots to have a sound sleep under shady trees, because a slight flow of wind would bring cool breeze. In the month of *Shravana*, the large rope swings would be hanged. Competitions on those large rope swings were organized every week. The person who could take the swing back and forth to the greatest height was declared the winner. Swinging in the rains gave the best of enjoyment. Rainbow after the rain created a scenic beauty – seen to be believed and enjoyed.

The name of our village was Rampur. People in the remote rural areas of the Punjab state were full of life. They drew the best of enjoyment from such competitions. In fact the immortal love stories of *Heer-Ranjha, Sohni-Mahiwal, Sasi-Poonu* and *Sahiba-Mirza* were afloat all around. Those love birds were the produce of the rural Punjab state, the area we belonged to. There were just 7 Muslim families. They were skilled workers in different trades. They were paid in kind for the whole year.

In the evening after reaching home, I told my father about the notice, I had written on my slate. There were no note-books. Our class teacher, Maulvi Khan Mohamed Baloch was a very good friend of my father. On way back home he used to play chess with my father. On the 12th of August evening they discussed about the notice. Khan Saheb was most revered teacher. He was in the school from the day of its inception.

He being a Baloch, was known/popular as *Pathan*. He used to wear white out-fits like a *pathan*. In today's times, he could be called "Mr. White", from head to toe. In the meantime other students had informed their parents. They were eagerly waiting to know the details of the discussions my father had with Khan Saheb. After he left for his home, people started coming to the *chowk*, the place of meetings. They were advised to go home, finish their dinner and re-assemble.

Partition of Our Country

Everybody went back, finished their dinner in a hurry and started re-assembling at the chowk. People had understood the matter was very serious. There was a lamp post. The lantern was lit. They could see each other. Normally children were not allowed to participate in such meetings of the elders. Since the matter was brought by us, the school going children, were allowed to sit in the middle, with strict instructions that we would not make any noise.

My father stood up narrated the deliberations of the discussions he had with Khan Saheb. He started saying, "On the earlier two occasions – The World War I and The World War II – we locked our houses and went to the places of safety. Many of us fought the wars to protect our country from outside invaders. They returned after the wars were over. We also returned to our houses. This time it would not be so. Our country has been divided into two parts. One would be called HINDUSTAN and the other as PAKISTAN. The date of this division would come into force on August 15, 1947. All Hindus will have to go to Hindustan, leaving our houses and house-hold goods here forever. All the Muslims would migrate to Pakistan."

Those days there were no newspapers in the remote areas and villages. First time I saw a newspaper in January 1946 at Lahore. It was known as the *Milap*. The medium of the script was Urdu. The other was the *Pratap*. The state was called the Punjab state. It extended up-to Haryana, Himachal Pradesh and Punjab. Its summer capital was Simla and in winters it was Lahore. In those days none of the families had radio in those remote areas. This type of news we did not get. Even the postman was coming to deliver the mail only once a week.

Since the matter was very serious we had to make decisions and take the necessary actions then and there. All the assembled people were advised to discuss the matter among themselves. Six or seven wise men met separately. They tried to understand the gravity of situation. After some time all the persons gathered again. One of the wise men started saying, "We have decided that we would not send our children to school from 13.8.1947 onwards". They suggested the following actions to be taken immediately:

1. We would leave for Hindustan on 15.8.1947.
2. Since there were no means of transportation, we would carry only such belongings which we could lift by ourselves.
3. If anybody from other villages wished to join us in our journey to Hindustan, they could come to Rampur anytime on August 13–14, 1947.
4. People at Rampur assured them that they would be looked after very well.
5. Those, who have cows/buffalos, were requested to bring those animals, so that there was no shortage of milk and butter for the children.
6. We should be prepared to face any situation. (Indirectly it was conveyed that if people had any weapon, it should be readily available for use).

   With those resolutions the meeting was dispersed.

It was pitch dark. People from other villages were provided *Lathis* to protect themselves from wild animals. Discussions at Rampur continued till mid-night. They had anticipated that Hindu families from other villages would start coming the next day morning itself.

It did happen. They started coming on 13 August morning and brought packages more than expected. We had a big house and accommodated 7 families having about 40 members (our own family consisted of 7 members). We also had 3 animals – 1 cow, 1 buffalos and 1 horse. On that day all the responsible persons became busy in arranging accommodation and meals. Ladies started grinding food-grains (wheat and Gram) on '*Chakki*' Stone (Flour Grinder). Big tandoors were made in each lane so that in one go 20 Chapattis could be cooked in every *tandoor*. By the time it was evening almost all the Hindu families from the nearby villages had reached Rampur. They ensured that all the guests were accommodated in different houses. However, the major problem they faced was to make arrangement for the morning/evening natural calls for the ladies and children. It was decided that they could go in groups before dawn and around sun-set in the evening. And husbands of some of the ladies would go as escorts.

Our father came home. He was completely exhausted. For children up-to our age, who did not understand, what our elders were talking about, it was like a festival (*Mela*), playing together and eating together. Nobody objected to our making noise.

My father had no time to have his lunch. He was forced to eat something. We all children, as the sun had already set, hurriedly finished our dinner and went out to play again.

Education System Then

It was then that my mother reminded my father that he had not made arrangements to bring back my elder brother from the hostel. He was in a middle school.

Those days there were 4 types of educational institutions.

1. Primary School – up-to Class 4. In 4th Class there used to be exam for scholarship. (Exam for Scholarship was optional and not compulsory)
2. Middle School – From 5th to 8th Class. 8th Class Exam was also used for Scholarships.
3. High School – up to Matriculation.
4. After matriculation, one year course called 'Prep' was compulsory to get admission in any college.
5. College Education could be completed in two Parts: 1. F.A/F.Sc./F.Com. 2. B.A/B.Sc/B.Com.
6. The Certificates for the respective parts were issued by the Punjab University, Simla.

Admission to a boy was given in the primary school in class 1 on his attaining the age of 6 years. Till then the boy used to learn certain things from his elders at home. Since majority of the families were farmers, the boys would drop out on completion of their primary school education. There was no such thing like Nursery, Lower KG and Upper KG schools. During these 6 years children would learn certain basic values of life by observing their elders' manners, how they behaved, how they talked and how they acted.

The first value of life the child would learn and would be taught was 'salutation'. This aspect the child was made to learn, when the child even did not know how to speak. It remains with the person till the rest of his/her life. It is preached and practiced throughout the world at large, irrespective of cast, creed, race, religion, sect, etc. In our country: East-West, North-South – the common practice is, we bow and touch the feet of our elders. It is not only a mark of respect, by touching the feet we resolve that we would keep on marching forward come what may. The second aspect is the child learns to recognize relationships. This also lives with us till the end of our life. Under certain circumstances some differences may crop up, but recognition of relationship remained.

Without formal education, the first 6 years of life are foundation stones of our life. In our Hindu philosophy there are 4 stages of life:

1. 01 to 25 years = Develop Strength and acquire Education
2. 25 to 50 years = Earn Wealth and raise Family
3. 50 to 75 years = Gradually pass on the responsibilities to other members and take a role of an adviser
4. 75 to 100 years = slowly renounce the world. Try to do selfless service. As the body becomes weak, devote more time to spiritual activities to attain *Moksha.*

Higher studies were done in the University. Syllabus and syllabus books were prescribed by the University. Once Books were selected and prescribed, they would remain in use for the following many years due to non-availability of material.

My elder brother, A.L. Budhiraja was studying in the middle school in another village – VASU ASTANA and he was put in the hostel. It was within the campus of the school. In early morning of August 14, 1947 one of our relative, Mr. Hari Chand Batra, with his horse, was sent to the hostel to bring my brother back home. On their arrival everybody was happy.

He (my brother) told us that their school had celebrated their Independence Day – YOME – E-AZADI – for PAKISTAN, by hoisting Pakistani National Flag. All the students were asked to be present to celebrate and salute the Pakistani flag. A well-known leader came to unfurl the flag. The students were instructed to say at the top of their voice: Pakistan Zindabad. After that the schools and colleges were closed for indefinite period.

Our Family

We were 7 members in the family then: father, mother, 2 sisters and 3 brothers. Our younger brother was just 10 months old. Our *Bhuaji* (fathers's sister) was a widow and was staying with us. She, after her husband died became a spiritual soul. During the day whenever she was free, she would take the spinning wheel to spin and the thread was kept aside. It was sold at a later date and the amount earned was handed over to her. She used to call it a '*Suchi Kamai*'. We had another premises – a portion of it was used by a saint-Mahatma. He would keep on repeating '*Sabhi Rang Tere*' at regular intervals, meaning thereby that whatever was happening, it was the will and wish of the Almighty God.

Once it so happened, that another Mahatma came. He would not eat at any body's house. He expressed that he would eat if the food was prepared out of '*Suchi Kamai*'. The amount earned by our *Bhuaji*, was used to buy material and food was cooked by my elder sister and was served to the Mahatma. The next day early morning He, the Mahatma, proceeded to his onward journey without seeing any body. This Mahatma had left a word with our Mahatma that he would never see such a pure and pious soul in his remaining life.

In the month of July, 1946 on a day in the late evening our Bhuaji asked our mother to make her bed. It was most unusual. She never allowed anybody to make her bed. She told our mother that she (our mother) was going to deliver a son. He should be named as Kishori Lal. She said she might not be there at the time of his birth. And she never woke up again from that bed. She left for her heavenly abode the same night.

Our father and mother were not educated. They had God given sense of understanding the matters. The problems put before them would be sorted out to the satisfaction of those who brought before them. Our father was a businessman – A successful business man. He used to buy standing crop in the field. He would go to meet the farmers on the field. Have a look on the standing crops: For wheat, grams and cotton – he kept first week of March every year. For maize, millet and sugarcane it was 1st week of August. He would analyze whose crop would produce how much? Which farmer would be easy to negotiate with? Who would look after the crop very well after the sale transaction was finalized? He would meet the pre-determined farmers, negotiate with them and confirm the deal orally. He would ask the farmer to meet him at his shop before the sunset. Take part/advance, of the agreed amount for which the farmer would put left thumb impression on the *Bahi-Khata* (Accounts Book).

The language and the figures used for maintaining the accounts could be understood by the business community people only. The condition for the farmer was that he had to look after the standing crop and ensure that animals, mouse and birds did not do any harm to the standing crop. He was very much considerate for the farmers. He was a man of few words. He was known for keeping his word even in the far distant places and was fondly addressed Choudhary Saheb. Some farmers would not take home the produce till he came and put first measure in the gunny bag. The measure was called TOPA (weighing 1 *Ser* – less than 1 Kg.), made of wood. This type of measures made of aluminum, can be seen and used by milk men even today, in different sizes: 100 ml, 250 ml, 500 ml and 1 litre.

Our mother was also blessed with some extra ordinary sense even at the young age. Our father had married twice. His first wife died when he was around 45 years of age. He had

3 daughters from his first wife. From our mother he had 8 children. After me there were 3 daughters, 2 died before partition and Sheela the 3rd one died in October 1947 before Diwali at Kurukhshetra. We could not get her treated by a doctor. She died of small pox.

Our mother was very strong spiritually. Those days there were no watches: wrist watch, alarm clock, wall clock in individual houses. The only wall clock with moving pendulum was in our school. In the morning, our mother would get up, by gazing the stars in the sky. There were no bathrooms in the house. She would take some more ladies for the natural calls and after that take bath on the well. She would do *puja* for nearly 1½ hours. By the time sun rose, she was on her regular routine work. Most of the times, we were looked after by our aunt and the eldest sister Shanti, daughter of our *Badi Maa*. She was married before partition and was at Khandawa in M.P. There were 2 more Budhiraja families. Brothers of our grandfather – Shri Devi Ditta Ram. One brother was fondly, called Baba Hem Raj and the other Baba Dharam Das. They too had big bungalows. Between our bungalow and Baba Hemraj's bungalow there was a double story bungalow. It had decorative fittings: doors, windows, walls, ceilings etc. Even the floor had glaring colored glazed tiles – a luxury in those days. Baba Dharam Das had brought those things, when he returned from the World War II.

During summers we all used to sleep on our terraces. On moonlit nights we could go to his terrace. He used to tell us stories about World Wars and the hardships he had undergone, the incidents of bravery, when fighting the enemy, how they enjoyed the days when there was no fighting. He had a loud voice. He would start reciting "*Jai Shiv Shambu, Bana Madiyan, Hata Tambu*" – the message was, there should be no wars, so that nobody has to stay in *Tambus* (Tents). In fact, the loud slogan, was an invitation for the children to join him at the terrace to enjoy the stories.

My elder brother was recognized as the most brilliant student right from the beginning. Whenever there was school inspection – once every year, the Head Master and teacher would ensure that he was present in the school. The teachers would ensure that no boy was absent on the inspection day. In his last year in the primary school (4th class, 1944) on the school inspection day he was not in a position to come to school. There was the river Jhelum's flood water near our school. We had to wade through the water to enter the school. The Head Master sent 3 boys, giving them his new bicycle (the only bicycle in 11 villages) to bring him to school. To cross flood water, he was physically lifted on the shoulders and brought to school. They had to climb the *Bund*. This *Bund* was constructed by the British Government. The land was fertile – the crop was wheat and cotton. It (the area of those remote villages) produced and provided strong men for the Army. Later on we learnt that Jhang district was rated as a backward district. However, in due course the people of district Jhang came to be considered as progressive. They were capable and adaptable to any change. They were the first in the country to initiate and adapt to widow marriage.

The river Jhelum was at a distance of about 15 kms from our village and 12 kms from the *Bund*. This distance of 12 kms was fixed keeping in mind that impact of the flood water would reduce by the time it reached *Bund*, and would not damage the Bund.

When the school Inspector came with his team, they took a round of the school. They were happy to see that school premises was well maintained. They were served a glass of hot milk with some dry fruit and dates (*Khajoor*). There was no such thing like tea. In fact we had not even heard about tea. Then the real inspection started. They started questioning the students. The medium of instructions was the Urdu language. He, my brother, used to write the answer on the slate. Unfortunately, he was not in a position to walk, he had to crawl to reach the Inspector with his answer. Every answer to their question was found to be correct. It was recorded in the inspection-book that our school was the only primary school in the district where the answers were 100% correct. In 1945 he was admitted in the middle school in another village called Vasu-Astana. His brilliance was observed by his new teachers as well. They were so much impressed that after the first quarterly exam, he was promoted to next class (6th std.).

It was difficult for me to step into his shoes. Teachers expected that in the school, I would take his place. I was always No. 2 in the class. No. 1 student in the class was one Mr. Shah from a nearby village. Incidentally, his father, my father and another person from our village were team members in a game. The game was played on every Thursday evening. The ground covered a large area. It was sufficient to construct 4 Stadiums of the modern age. The game was played by the men of very strong physique, high stamina and very fast runners. Average height of the participants was around 6 feet. Many a times the players suffered fatal injuries. My father once broke his left arm elbow.

Sometimes competitions were held among teams from different villages. The winning team was awarded a *Pagadi* (signifying the symbol of the greatest honor) to each member of the team. It was the most entertaining game. For children it was a feast day. The field was not viable for crop production but best suited as a playground. It was in close proximity to *Thar desert.* In the desert there was a sand hillock. On the top of that hill there was a tree. It was unbelievable to see a green leafy tree in a desert. The sand hillock was known as *Majnu-ka-Tilla*. It was useful for those who passed through the desert, as a compass.

For our recess tiffin we used to take dry fruits: almonds, walnuts, pine nuts, and on some days we carried dry fruits stuffed thick hard bread using jaggery or sugar. We both the brothers used to get pocket money and were allowed to eat any junk food.

My younger sister – Sheela – was also a pious soul. In the afternoon, there used to be satsang in our house. Many ladies used to come in the satsang. At the tender age of 5 she would make all the arrangements – brooming the place, laying the mats and arranging drinking water. The persons who came to attend the satsang were amazed to see arrangements made flawlessly. They used to bless her.

14.8.1947 was a day of activity for the responsible wise-men. They had received requests, rather threats from the Muslim heads of the villages, to send back the Hindu families, from where the Hindus had come to Rampur. The male members of the families shifted to Rampur on 13th and 14th were requested to come to the Chowk. The messages received from their villages were discussed and they were asked to decide. Only some families of one village decided to go back. On their crossing the nearby rivulet, they were looted by masked men. They ran back for the safety of their life. There was emergency meeting, what they had anticipated had happened. It was decided to protect the village during the night. Four teams were made. Each team would have 4 strong men. They would be replaced after 4 hours by another team of 4 members.

On the morning of 14.8.1947 – the day of YOME-E-AZADI for Pakistan, our teacher Khan Saheb went to school to celebrate and hoist the Pakistan's National Flag on that special day. On his way back from the school my father met him and apprised him about the developments. He stayed in our village till the sunset.

After the sunset some men went to their homes in their villages to protect their home and the cattle. At around 10.00 o'clock in the night, they were attacked. Men at Rampur could hear their cries and shouts for help. Many young and strong men with weapon and a lantern ran to the direction from where cries were heard. The wounded were brought back to Rampur. They were treated by the *vaidyas* with available herbs. In some cases wounds were deep and they were unable to walk. It was very obvious that the next day – 15.8.1947 was going to be tough and a horrible day. Another decision taken was that we all should be in the houses in the middle of the village, so that in any such eventuality, we could help each other. Four inter-connected buildings were identified, where all the persons were to assemble.

Swatantrata Divas/Independence Day August 15, 1947

Finally the fateful day – August 15, 1947 – arrived. My elder brother told us that in Hindustan it would be known as *Swantrantra Divas.* As decided on the previous day, everybody ate morning meal/break-fast: *bajra* chapatis, fresh butter/ mango pickles and big full glass of butter-milk as much as they could drink and everybody in Rampur assembled in those 4 buildings. All those persons who were attacked the previous night were also brought and fresh dressing was done. Only our grand uncle, Baba Dharam Das and his wife Amma Dui did not come. They were very weak and frail. Our father met them. They told him that their days were numbered. He had done enough for them and they would love to die in their own home. They did not want to be a burden on anybody any more. They had daughters and all were married.

15.8.1947 was being celebrated in Hindustan – as *Swantantra Divas.* We were undergoing the untold miseries. The sky was over-cast. It gave us a relief from the scorching sun heat. Around 10:00 o'clock we could see many muscle men fully armed had gathered near our village and many more were coming to join them from different directions. That sent a dreadful wave of fear. It could be seen on everybody's face. Incidentally, all the ladies and the small hildren were inside the houses.

The wise men met again to decide the next course of action to be taken to face those people assembled. Unfortunately the leader of those muscle-men was a member of the team in the game they played and the 3rd member was from our village. On 14.8.1947 evening my father had handed over all the cattle to him to look after them and keep sending us the milk. He was sent for and a message was sent to Mr. Shah that Choudhry Saheb along with some other respectable people wanted to meet him to discuss certain matters. The leader of the large number of armed men gathered there, agreed for the meeting near the corner of the village.

All the members of the team of wise-men plus 3 strong, well-built young men went to participate in the meeting. The 3rd team member being the common friend accompanied them. About 10 persons from the 'invaders' came. Some cots were brought. They knew each other very well. They exchanged pleasantries with smiling faces, and without hard feeling. The way they were sitting together, it could not even be perceived that they could be from two different camps. The discussions started in a very cordial atmosphere. The discussions continued for nearly 45 minutes. Barring one, all the points discussed, were agreed upon. The one point not accepted was that a head of a village Khiluwala wanted two persons – Dwarka Das and Ramlal – Father and Son – of a family from his village be handed over to him. He had enmity with them.

The following points agreed upon were:

1. They would protect us from all those who would try to harm/attack us.
2. For all those present there then, would be paid Rs. 2,000/- as compensation and Mr. Shah would distribute the amount and would ensure that everybody would get his share.
3. Everyone present there would be served pure *ghee halva.*

As agreed upon Rs. 2000/- from all the families were collected. It was a voluntary contribution. Any shortfall was covered up by the persons who could afford to contribute more. Like-wise *Atta*, pure ghee, sugar and milk along with utensils and fire wood to cook *halva* were arranged, so that they could cook *halva* themselves. They enjoyed the feast. By then it was afternoon.

Suddenly, an unfortunate incident took place. They sighted a police man at a distance from our village. They felt, they were double crossed. The Hindus had sought government help and the Hindus did not reveal that fact to them. Mr. Shah rushed on his horse with a spear in his hand. He challenged the police man. The person was not actually a police man. He was an Imposter. They discussed something and imposter returned back. Mr. Shah returned shouting *Looto* (pick up anything you can), *Marrow/Kato* (kill them show no mercy). It was unbelievable reaction of his after meeting the police man. On south-west side of the village some houses were set on fire. They entered the village and started pelting stones. It was horrifying. Ladies and children started crying. It was horrifying, because only a few hours earlier, as agreed, they were to protect us, and now they were acting as terrorists. There was no time for discussion. It was immediately decided that instead of getting burnt in these houses, everyone should go out in the open outside the village. Some men requested the invaders that we were allowed to go out in the open towards the Bund.

They accepted our request. They stopped pelting stones. All of us, children, ladies, men – young and old started running out of the building. It was like a stampede. Nobody knew where the other family members were. Most of us even did not get chance to wear our shoes and ran bare foot. Out of fear, some children and ladies started crying. Some men tried to bring out men who were injured on 14.8.1947 night at their villages. At the fag end of the stampede both, Sh. Dwarka Das and Ramlal who were injured seriously and were unable to walk properly were sighted by the person who demanded them during the discussion in the morning. He along with his accomplices caught hold of both of them. The hatred of the years over powered them and the cruelty erupted. Both the father and son were hanged upside-down. They started piercing their body with the tips of spears and swords. It was a gruesome torture. The painful cries and yells could be heard from a distance. That provoked the other terrorists present there. They started shouting ALLAH-HU-AKBAR. That created a horrifying atmosphere.

After coming out we kept on running and by the time those pathetic cries were heard, we had reached near the Bund. At a distance of about 2 km. a village called Loharu was protected by the Muslims there and the Hindus of Loharu had not come to Rampur on 13th or 14th August. We were being chased like herds. We both the brothers were running side by side. On crossing the Bund we looked back to locate where our parents and sisters were. We saw our father had lifted our younger sister Sheela on his shoulders. Our elder sister Bhiranwan was not far behind. It was our mother with our small kid brother (10 months old) in her arms completely exhausted. My elder brother tried to help her. She encouraged him – "Keep running, I will manage". In the meantime some persons who were far behind were attacked by the terrorists. Since the sky was over cast right from the morning we were relieved of burning heat of sun.

We were near Loharu and men at Loharu heard our noises. They assumed that some persons from other villages were going to attack their village. They came out fully equipped with arms. We reached near the village and they saw ladies and children. They came running to help us. The terrorists, seeing the men from Loharu did not dare to confront them. They turned back.

It was possibly around 4:00 o'clock in the evening. We were nearly seven hundred people. They came to know we had not eaten anything since morning. The ladies started preparing *chapattis* and *dal.* Some of our ladies joined them in the community kitchen. Rice was not part of our regular food. People rested for some time. It rained in the late evening. After the sunset, it was pitch dark. The rain had stopped. The terrorists came there in large number. They threatened the leader and the protector of the village of Loharu to throw out all Hindus who had come from Rampur. The brave man succumbed to the pressure. He returned, gathered all the Hindu responsible persons. He conveyed what the intruders wanted. It was dreadful.

Fear could be seen on the face of one and all. People from Loharu felt for us. Everybody had one question "In that dark cloudy night where would we go for shelter?" We had no option. He was assured that we, who came from Rampur, would leave soon. He went back and told the terrorists that the Hindus from Rampur have started leaving. The terrorists rushed to chase us once again. The darkness came to our rescue and once again we were separated from our families.

My cousin, Vanti Devi about 6–7 years elder to me held my hand tightly. Both of us hid in a nearby sugar cane field. Due to rain a couple of hours ago, the field was full of water. We had to stand. Sugar cane had gained good height, so we could not be spotted in the darkness. After some time hearing no voice from any side we started moving to come out of the field. Due to water we were moving cautiously. In the process both of us moved in the different directions. Finding myself all alone in the darkness I started trembling with fear. I was about to cry, I hit the pavement. I realized I am out of the sugar cane field full of water. Slowly I walked on the pavement. I was in the open. The clouds were not so dark. I could see the passage and saw a house at some distance and the fear in me reduced. Somebody from behind caught hold of me and pushed me into the room. Some more persons were already in that room. Immediately my mouth was covered with a piece of cloth. The room in fact was a cattle shed. It was stinking. Rain water was dripping from the roof into the room. Mouths of small children were tightly held covered with cloth, so that cries or screaming was not heard outside the room. At around midnight, Mr. Ganpat Taneja and Mr. Vidya Sagar of Loharu came to inform us that most of the persons were safe. They had brought milk to feed the children.

At that very moment somebody came to inform that an injured lady was lying in a nearby field. She was brought fully drenched in mud. On seeing her I was stunned. I caught hold of my mother tightly and started sobbing. She was my cousin – Vanti who protected me only a few hours ago. She was hit by a sharp weapon in the head. Due to thick hair the injury was not very deep. My mother requested the owner of the house to bring a scissors. Hair around her injury were cut, some *haldi* (Turmeric) and ash was applied on the injured part. It was covered with leaves and a bandage was tied. After sometime she gained consciousness. Everyone present there heaved a sigh of relief. She enquired about me, she was told that I was safe and was there. Since the sky had cleared mats were brought and ladies and children were advised to sleep. Young and strong men volunteered to keep awake. Three groups were made and after every two hours the group would be replaced. Thankfully there was no rain on that night.

This was how we celebrated our *Swatantra Divas,* 15th August 1947 – surrounded by friends and foes.

On August 16th 1947 we got up in the morning fearlessly as if nothing had happened during the last 4 days. No clouds, no rains and bright sunny day. We saw 2 young and strong men. They were sons of Mr. Saiyal. Saiyals proved to be the real friends in need. They had come to guard and protect us from terrorists. We youngsters went to the nearby field. Previous day's rain water had completely dried up. Next to the field there was a canal not very wide where rain water was running. We boys decided to enjoy swimming. The tall boys jumped into the canal and tried to see how deep the water was. It was just chest deep level. They allowed us to join them with a warning that we would not enter the deep water and would not go far away from each other. We had no clothes to change except those we had worn on 15th August morning. We entered the canal naked – without any underwear. We came back. Children were given milk and elders were offered different varieties of *Khajoor* (dates) freshly plucked from the trees.

We did not think even for a moment, under what strain and stress our parents were passing through. Our ladies would not take any cooked food from the Muslim's kitchen. They, our protectors – Ms. Saiyals, had provided wheat and gram. Salt and other spices were brought from Hindu families of Loharu along with 3-4 grinding stones to make wheat *atta*. Some Hindu ladies had started making *atta*, because for 2 meals – lunch and dinner – for so many persons at least 100 kg. *atta* was required. Temporary *Tandoors* and cooking stove were made by digging the ground. The community kitchens were ready. Ladies made chapatis and men cooked grams. Every Hindu family would make at least 10 to 15 kg of mango pickle during mango season and 2–3 kg. green and red chillis' pickles. No meal was complete without pickle.

This type of scene of eating together in a large of number of people could be witnessed only on some special functions or marriages. It amounted to unplanned celebration of our Independence – missing the hoisting of our national flag. Unfortunately, majority of us even did not know how our national flag looked like. We had seen flags at temples, gurudwaras and mosques, but it was a unique flag having different colors.

Fortunately for us, we had a chance to see – Tiranga Jhanda – our national flag at Lahore. In January, 1946 after 14th January, there was marriage of our cousin, Mr. V.D. Dev, son of our Bhua Mehran. She was the eldest sister of our father. She had 4 sons and a daughter. Two elder sons, Mr. Chiman Lal and Mr. Ladha Ram and the daughter had already married. Mr. V.D. Dev was getting married. He was the chief editor of a daily Urdu newspaper – The Milap. He told us about the Independence movement by our leaders to get India free from British rule. Our young heroes: Sardar Bhagat Singh and his associates sacrificed their lives in that freedom movement. He also told us about the atrocities inflicted on our freedom fighters by the British rulers. There we had a chance to see our national flag.

There we also learnt about the celebration of the festival of *Lohari/Uttrayan*. It falls on January 14th in every calendar year. From our Bhuaji's grandsons, Somnath and Om Prakash, who were of our age, we learnt a particular folk song sung on that festival. We participated in it and enjoyed the festival with zeal and zest. It was a great experience and entertainment for us. On that festival night many folk songs were sung in praise of the heros: Bhagat Singh and his associates and fiancée of Bhagat Singh.

Coming back, the marriage party was to go to Gojara. It was yet another experience for us. From Lahore to Gojara we travelled by bus. We children occupied back seats to enjoy our own pranks. It was a sunny-windy day. The road was not wide. Time and again the dust would come into the bus. We did not shut the windows. Sunshine was a relief from the cold of

January. By the evening, we reached Gojara and my white shirt and half pant gathered lot of dust. I was feeling uncomfortable. A grand reception was accorded to the marriage party. For us coming from a remote small village everything was a first time experience. My elder sister Lajvanti and brother-in-law Mr. Shiv Dayal lived in Gojara. They were also invited. On seeing them I felt very much comfortable. After marriage dinner I went with them to stay for the night.

We both, father and son, came back from Gojara to Rampur. We reached Rampur in the late evening. It was complete dark in the streets of Rampur. A dim light of a lamp was peeping out of the doors of *Panditaiyen* Ramkauran. On reaching home first thing I did was to clean my *Takthi* (a wooden board) and apply *Multani Mitti* to make it bright and smooth to write some lines in Urdu. It was done to practice and improve beautiful hand-writing. The ink used was homemade, by adding certain ingredients that would make it shine to give shining appearance of the written matter. The next day morning I wrote on the board "*Aaye The Hum Sair Karne, Sair Gulshan Kar Chuke, Dekh Maali Baugh Apna Hum To Apne Ghar Chale*". It was a daily home work. Medium of instruction was Urdu. Official language was also Urdu. The only language which was unique in quality when writing a letter (alphabet) a part of it is sleek and thin up to a point followed by a broad part yet again followed by sleek and thin line. The writer could use his skill that the full word appealed to the reader.

Lahore was a beautiful city. It was known as city of fashions. Any new fashion emanated first, from Lahore. There was a famous saying 'If a person had not seen Lahore, he/she was not born'. Both the brothers – Somnath and Om Prakash were born and brought up in a big city Lyalpur (after the partition the name of the city was changed to Faizalabad). On our way to Lahore we stayed at Lyalpur for 2 days. Somnath and Om Prakash were sons of Mr. Ladharam. Lyalpur was a well planned city. It had very wide roads. In the heart of the city, there was a clock tower (*Ghanta Ghar*) having a height of about 60 to 70 feet. It could be seen from far of distance. In certain areas, the buildings were of the shape of a square. The buildings were having 3 to 4 storeys and would accommodate 5 to 6 families, on each floor and the open space was in the middle of the building, open space was connected with iron rods. The logic for such buildings was: 1) The fresh air and sun-light would pass through that open space and would reach right up to ground floor. 2) To protect if anything or anybody fell down and no damage was caused. Most important feature we noticed was that on each floor, arrangements were made for natural calls and taking bath. Water was drawn by hand pumps. Nearly 100 persons living in building, for us it was amazing because the space covered by our house having 9 persons and 3 cattle was bigger than the area of that building accommodating 100 persons. It was full of life till mid night.

While coming to Lahore, we travelled by bullock-carts in the night from Layalpur. It was common mode of traveling. It formed a convoy of 25 carts. Each cart was pulled by 2 bulls. In the neck of each bull there was a leather belt with 6 or 8 bells made of brass. Under the cart behind the bulls, there was a lantern swinging back and forth. Between 4 carts there was a dog. With the movement of bulls the bells would ring and produce a musical tune, as if it was composed by an artist. At the turn of the road the light of lanterns would take a shape of twinkling necklace. At that age we did not appreciate the scenic beauty, we were experiencing. As the night fell, we youngsters were fast asleep. The next day we reached our destination Lahore.

They, Som Nath and Om Prakash, took us to show different parts worth seeing in Lahore. Many men from Kabul and

Baluchistan used to come to Lahore in search of job. Their dress was typical. They were lively persons and lived care free life. They were hard working and trustworthy persons. They were lively persons and in spite of day's hard work, they enjoyed their life by singing their native folk songs and dancing.

Coming back to the present, on 16th August 1947 morning it was noticed that some members of certain families were missing. Men of those families along with the responsible team members (team formed at Rampur) went to the village Loharu to ascertain whether any missing person was there and unfortunately there was none. It was concluded that they had either been killed or kidnapped. What was more painful was that under the prevailing conditions the grieved members of the families were not allowed to cry to express their grief. People around them consoled them in a hushed voice. It was an unbearable heartbreaking pain.

Otherwise, the day of 16th August 1947 passed off well. It was peaceful without any untoward incident. We children played, played and played under the shady trees. Our elders were less stressful outwardly, internally they were shattered. After lunch the team members and some more men went to the village again, met Mr. Ganpat and other Hindu wise men. Discussed various aspects and what should be the next course of action.

They did not want the Hindus in Loharu should suffer, because of the Hindu families from Rampur hiding there. As majority of the missing persons, observed in that morning, were ladies, they decided to fight back with the terrorists. They enquired from the men of Loharu if they had some extra weapons. If they had, could they lend some for a couple of days? They agreed to spare some. They returned accompanied by Mr. Ganpat. The Muslim brave man Mr. Saiyal, who had provided us shelter, was briefed about the discussions and the decision to fight back the terrorists, if they reappeared. He and his sons assured us their full support.

On 17th August 1947 we were forced to wake up before dawn. The previous day a dreadful decision was made by our elders to protect the chastity of women, they should be killed and thrown into the river Jhelum, then fight the terrorists fiercely, so that we did not die a cowardly death. That resolve was not revealed to women and children. The weapons brought from Loharu were handed over to the men. Even the kids like us were also given a tool (*Dranti*) used to cut the crop or grass, in case of need it should be used as a weapon fearlessly. We were encouraged by our parents that were capable and strong enough to hit back the terrorists. From the heart of hearts nobody wanted it to happen.

All of us started to march towards the river Jhelum. We had hardly reached the nearby canal, we heard loud voices 'Allaha-Hu-Akbar'. At some distance, it was noticed that a large number of terrorists were coming. Another decision (suggested by our well-wisher – the brave Muslim protector) was made, "In the event, we did not get a chance to execute our plan, the ladies, children and elderly persons would take shelter in the Mosque". Accordingly, all of us including men took shelter in the nearby mosque and were saved from a massacre. The terrorists, due to their religious compulsions, did not dare to enter the mosque and went back. The Hindus of Loharu served us lunch, near the mosque.

By the time we finished our lunch, a Muslim friend (a very good friend) of our father, came and assured him full protection, if we go with him to his village. In a good gesture, he was given ear rings and bangles of our mother the only ornaments our mother was wearing. He, with those ornaments, went away and never returned.

Another village called, Dosa, was protected by Mr. Ishtefaq Ahmad Qureshi. Our close relatives, Mr. Chokha Ram, his brothers Ladha Ram, Karam Chand and other 20 family members and many more Hindu families lived there. Somehow, a message was sent to our relatives about the stress and strain we were undergoing. By evening before the sunset 5 men on their horses from Dosa came to Loharu to take us (7 of us plus 3 of our cousins' family members). We were much relieved and started going with them. Before starting our father went and thanked the Muslim fried Mr. Saiyal who protected us during the last 3 days and also expressed his gratitude to Mr. Ganpat and all other Hindus for their help and support. Some other Hindu families of Rampur started following us. Majority of us were bare foot. The passage we were walking on, there were thorns, because of which many of us started bleeding. Around midnight the moon appeared spreading moonlight and we could see the passage clearly. The girls of our age even elder to us were dead tired. We had no option, we had to walk some more distance, around 1 km.

Covering some more distance our guards declared that they were advised to bring only 10 persons and not more. Our father requested them to go and convey Mr. Qureshi and Mr. Chokha Ram that Choudhry Chela Ram wanted to talk to them. They along with our cousins were waiting for us and were worried as to why we had not reached Dosa. Receiving the message both Mr. Qureshi and Mr. Chokha Ram came. Our father asked Mr. Chokha Ram, if we had to feed these many people, at least 2 meals a day, for how long we could feed them? Mr. Chokha Ram assured that there was enough to feed these many persons for a minimum of 6 months. He (our father) looked up to Qureshi Saheb and said "we would meet your day to day requirements, you protect us from the terrorists".

In the meantime, some families, who had come with us, had moved to another nearby village called Jhakhian. It was also protected by Muslims and Hindus jointly. Our cousins, Shri Ganesh Das, his wife, sister and the younger brother Nathu Ram had gone straight to Dosa from Rampur. Mr. Nathu Ram's wife was with us. After we reached Dosa their family was also complete. There was nobody missing.

18th August 1947 morning was a pleasant morning. When we got up we did not believe ourselves that we slept the whole night without even a mattress. The sound sleep was due to: 1) the assurance that we had reached a place where we were safe. 2) We were dead tired of the fear experienced in the morning at Loharu and then covering a long distance bare foot till midnight of 17th August 1947.

It appeared miseries had decided not to allow us to have peace of mind. The news of missing women of Rampur had reached Dosa on 16.8.1947 itself. Mr. Karam Chand, younger brother of Shri Chokha Ram was affected so much by that news that he took a draconian action that a normal person would not even think of such an action. He asked all the women of their family to come to the nearby well. He dumped them in a room near the well. He brought them out one by one. Beheaded them and threw them into the well. The only person he did not kill was his mother but pushed her into the well alive. Afterwards he tied his own legs and hands and pushed himself into the well. All of them died except the old lady (mother). All the dead bodies were cremated on 17.8.1947. This cruel act was enacted to protect the chastity of women of the family. That act had shaken everybody in the village. The shock and fear was visible and could be seen as shadow of death.

The courage to maintain the balance of mind, after the massacre and cremation of so many members of the family, exhibited by Shri Chokha Ram and his friend Mr. Ishtefaq Qureshi was not only exemplary, it was unparalleled. All the 5 persons, who had come to pick us up, allowed their emotions not to appear on their faces during the period we walked from Loharu to Dosa. It was only when my father and Shri Chokha Ram together were all alone Shri Chokha Ram broke down. He could not control his emotions. Our father too was moved. He also could not control his emotions. Both of them were very large hearted persons, both cried like children. The gap created by destiny was unbridgeable. Both of them accepted the painful and irrepairable loss. About that heart breaking casualties, everybody came to know on 18th morning itself. Some ladies started crying. They were advised to control their cries. The feelings they wanted to express should be limited to sobbing only, without any loud voice.

18th August, 1947 did not give us any respite. Both the friends taking the help of Mr. Qureshi were busy in making the arrangements for stay and food to be provided to so many persons. Ladies and children were accommodated in the houses of Hindu families. Men were advised to take some rest under the shady trees. Mr. Qureshi extended his full co-operation and support. Incidentally, Mr. Qureshi's son, Mushtaque Ahmed was also studying in the same middle school at Vasu-Astana and was staying at the same hostel, where my elder brother – Aenshi Lal was staying. Elder boys made their own group. They started playing volleyball in the evening. The day passed off with grief filled hearts and lifeless activities. Everybody prayed that the souls of the slained persons rested in peace. During the day, arrangements were made by raising tents normally used for marriages and other functions, so that men could also get some sleep.

On 19th August we came to know that at Dosa yet another family of Mr. Kalu Ram Batra was completely eliminated. His wife and 2 daughters were being whisked away. Both the father and son dared to face them even both the daughters mustered their courage. The terrorists more in number killed all the 5 members of the family of Mr. Kalu Ram. That sad episode had shaken all of us at heart.

On 20th August, we had to face a critical situation. Mr. Ishtafaq Qureshi's brother had taken loan from us against some gold ornaments. In the month of February, 1947 our father had gone to Lahore to attend the marriage of our cousin Mr. S.L. Dev. He had taken some cash to keep a deposit in the bank. One of our distant relative at Dosa somehow got this information. He went and talked to Mr. Qureshi advised him to demand his ornaments. Those days it was known practice that all the valuables were hidden in the walls.

Iron cupboard/safes were a rarity and luxury. Though we had a very heavy cupboard (around 1000 kg.), we had also followed the practice of keeping valuables in the walls. When the cupboard was brought to take it in the main hall, the doors and door-frame were removed and afterwards re-fixed. The valuables were put in to the earthen pot and then the wall was constructed in the normal manner. Since all communities: Hindus, Muslims and Sikhs used the same method, they knew where the valuables could be. After we were chased away in the evening, our houses were ransacked. Even the firewood stored for winter season had been taken away. The 7 families who had been accommodated in our house had also dumped some articles underground. The whole compound was dug like a field and all valuables and house-hold goods were taken away.

On Mr. Qureshi's demand to return his ornaments, our father was initially frightful. He had no choice. Our father explained to Mr. Qureshi in presence of Mr. Chokharam the location where the ornaments were buried. The pot also contained some of our own ornaments. The location was under a window between the house and shop. Our shop and the main hall of our house were connected by a window. As a general practice as there was no watch or clock, the closing times of the shop was fixed as sunset. After sunset if a customer came to buy something it was sold by getting the item through the window. This practice was followed for years, so the surface of the window became very very hard. The intruders must have tried their best to dig the surface of the window. Finally, they gave up the idea and left the surface un-dug assuming that there was nothing hidden in this window.

In the afternoon of 21st August, 1947, 6 persons, 3 from Mr. Qureshi's family and our father and 2 relatives of Mr. Chokha Ram went to Rampur on their horses fully armed to combat any attack by the terrorists. In the evening, when they reached Rampur, they were stunned. The shop was a shelter place of the dogs. Everything was looted including the wooden cash box and the weighing scale and weights. To build the home and the shop it took years and to turn it in to a dogs hide out, it took just 6 days! It was unbearable scene. With the main objective in mind all of them entered the shop. Seeing the window our father had a sigh of relief. He called all the members who had come for purpose and pointed out the place where the ornaments were buried. Seeing the surface of the window he said that it seems the miscreants had not succeeded in getting those ornaments.

The window surface was dug. They had to work very hard to bring out the pot containing ornaments. The pot was opened. Before leaving Dosa our father had discussed all details with Mr. Qureshi. He had brought an inkpot and a piece of paper. Two separate lists were made: One for the ornaments of Mr. Qureshi and the other for our own ornaments. It was also decided that pot containing ornaments would be handed over to Mr. Chokha Ram's brother-in-law. Our father went around the house. He found nothing to carry. He remembered that there was a wall which had a crack and on 15.8.1947 morning my mother had taken out her chain she was wearing and pushed it in to the crack. He quietly took out that chain from the crack. That was the treasure he could retrieve from his home.

Before returning from Rampur our father went to Baba Dharam Das's house. As expected both Baba Dharam Das and Amma Dui were lying dead. There was nothing to cremate them. They were buried and their own home became the graveyard for them. All 6 of them prayed to the almighty god for their souls to rest in peace. With the anxiety he had come from Dosa, he felt relieved now for 1. Mr. Qureshi's ornaments were found intact. 2. He could perform some last rite of his elders (Uncle and Aunt).

Mission Rampur was completed successfully. They reached Dosa and the sun was setting. In those turbulent days it was considered risky to keep away from home after sunset. Mr. Qureshi and Mr. Chokha Ram were waiting for their return. Both of them were briefed about the completion of mission Rampur. Mr. Chokha Ram's brother-in-law handed over the pot full of ornaments to Mr. Chokha Ram. Mr. Ishtefaq Qureshi was very happy to receive back his brother's ornaments. He paid us Rs. 1100/- out of Rs. 1400/- the amount of loan he had taken. He exhibited his greatness. Even if he had not paid any amount we would have been happy because he had protected us from terrorists and saved our lives. The amount paid to us was worth millions. We were penny less. We were unable to arrange shoes for ourselves and slippers for the ladies. We were going bare-foot for the last 6 days. The first thing we did was to order 3 pairs of shoes and 3 pairs of slippers for the ladies to be delivered to us by 22.8.1947 evening.

Mr. Chokha Ram, Ladha Ram, their brother-in-law and son-in-law and the ladies who survived had not come out of grief caused by the loss of lives of so many family members. The courage and patience they had shown by accommodating and serving us all was unparalleled. Out of seven hundred persons nearly 400 had gone to other villages: Jhakhiyan, Khanewal, Chhona and some remained at Loharu. Jhakhiyan was the village where our 3rd Bhua – Parvati lived. On 21.8.1947 evening a big number of terrorists came to Dosa and threatened Mr. Ishtefaq Qureshi to send away all the Hindus who had come from Rampur. Mr. Ishtefaq Qureshi was a man of guts and courage. He sent the message that they (terrorists) dare not misadventure to enter or harm people at Dosa. They were under his protection. They would continue to be here till the government made the required arrangements to send them to Hindustan.

In the meantime, all Hindus ran to take shelter in the mosque. We started reciting Muslim prayer (*Kalma*) in the mosque (*La-Illa-Il-Lla Muhamad-Ul-Rasul-Illa*). It was a question of survival. Mr. Ishtefaq's words worked. They (terrorists) did not do any misadventure of entering Dosa, and went back. We came out of the mosque after the sunset and receiving the message from Qureshi Saheb. For, we children, it had become a matter of amusement. Another favorable point was that there was no rain during the 4 previous days.

On 23.8.1947 we came to know that the government had made a camp for all those Hindus who have been displaced from their homes. They could come and stay in the camp under the protection of army. All other daily needs would also be taken care of in the camp. The camp was located at Thana Atharanzari, a bigger village. It was made a temporary cantonment.

Mr. Qureshi wanted to be sure whether the news was correct. He sent his men to nearby village to confirm if they had received the similar news. He had also sent a person to Thana Atharanzari to get the authentic information. The man had gone on a horse. He gathered the required information and reached back in the evening before sunset. Responsible persons from Dosa and Hindus of Rampur assembled to decide the next course of action to be taken. After a lengthy discussion the following resolutions were passed:

1. All Hindus from Rampur and from Dosa would be sent to Thana Atharanzari camp in two batches.
2. Camels' carts would be hired to transport all the persons and we would bear all the expenses. Mr. Qureshi also arranged some escorts to accompany each batch.
3. To avoid any confrontation with anybody the camels would leave us at some distance from the camp.
4. The escorts would return after ensuring that all of us had been allowed to enter the camp.
5. The required number of camel carts would be arranged by 25.8.1947.
6. First batch would start after sunset immediately after taking the dinner. The 2nd batch would start after some time so that there was not much gap between the two.

We reached Thana Atharanzari camp in the morning of 26.8.1947. One family at a time was sent to the camp to take entry. For the first batch the entry into the camp was smooth. For the second batch, the *sentry* at the gate became strict and rigid. He was requested and informed that people had walked a long distance to reach the camp to get protection. Finally, he agreed to take everybody into the camp. The camel carts and the escorts were paid the amount to their satisfaction. Our father told us that they had mixed feelings on their faces – smile and sorrow.

Mixed feelings were in our hearts too:

1. Terrorists would not dare to chase us anymore.
2. Army personnel were more dependable to protect us. Many persons from our village had fought in the World War I and World War II and how they helped the needy people.
3. There were thousands of people displaced like us in the camp.
4. As was visualized on 12.8.1947, we would never return to our homes.
5. We were identified as 'Refugees'.

We were allotted a tent for 7 persons. Our father then went to arrange milk for our younger sister and brother. Many people had come in the meantime to join the camp. On his return with a pot of milk our father was not allowed to enter the camp. When he pleaded, the sentry got angry and broke the pot of milk. Another Army man came to his rescue and granted him permission to enter the camp. He returned empty handed. He narrated the whole incident. For a 10 months old child milk was a necessity. He decided to make another attempt to arrange milk for the child. In the next tent a lady had heard the incident narrated by our father. Fortunately, some milk was lying unused with them. She gave that milk to us. Our mother offered her money for the milk. She did not accept money saying, "we have also undergone that type of humiliation during the last 3 days."

Lunch was provided by army in the camp itself. People in the next tent and our family developed good understanding. It was decided that each family would go for lunch turn by turn. The reason was, the tents were in short supply and tent if found empty could be allotted to another family.

The inflow of refugees was swelling. To provide better facilities and avoid inconvenience to the people in the camp, the army had decided, that people should be shifted to another camp on regular basis. On the morning of 28.8.1947, the people in the next tent were advised to come to the exit door of the camp. They were to go to another camp. To shift people the army had arranged army trucks. We also boarded the truck. Our mother had handed over 10 months old Kishorilal and as she was trying to climb the truck, it moved. She fell down and got hurt. All of us and other in the truck started shouting to stop it. The driver appeared to be considerate. He not only stopped the truck, he backed it. Our mother was lifted to enter the truck. By afternoon we reached the next refugee camp – *Heer-ka-maqbara*. It was a very big camp, having a high boundary wall. We were allotted a tent. It was smaller in size in comparison to the one allotted to us at Thana Atharanzari.

The army had made all arrangements for a comfortable stay. A blanket was supplied. We used it as a mattress. Ladies slept inside the tent and the gents slept in front of the tent. The army personnel were there to protect us, we slept fearlessly.

On 29.8.1947 morning we found for natural calls separate arrangements were made for ladies and gents. Similarly, for taking bath hand pumps were installed separately. For meals service also there were 2 queues – one for ladies and for the gents. They ensured everybody in the camp took meals.

In the afternoon of 29.8.1947 it rained heavily. We children started playing and enjoying in the rain. We had no other clothes to change. Our parents were concerned about us, so that we did not catch cold. They advised us to come into the tent. The water was drained out first from shirt and then from salwar. We had no option but wear wet clothes. By the sunset, rain stopped. We were advised to dry the clothes one-by-one in the air. It was forcible cleansing of clothes after 5 days. On

30.8.1947 it again rained. It continued for nearly 4–5 hours. It caused a concern in the army management camp. The cause of concern was that there were thousands of people in the camp and if any infectious disease broke out, it would be disastrous. They made some emergency arrangements to cope up in any such situation.

Heer-Mai-ka-Maqbara was at the other end of the compound. The next day, we heard, people talking that in spite of such heavy rains there was not a drop of water on the *maqbara.* It was a miracle. We missed the chance of witnessing such a miracle. In any case it was a- hear say, there was no evidence to prove its authenticity. The days passed by, peacefully under the protection of the army personnel. The refugees from different parts of district Jhang were coming every day. To accommodate additional families in the camp, the families who had come 7–8 days earlier were shifted to Jhang Mandi (wholesale market) of Jhang city. We were shifted to Jhang Mandi camp.

On 3.9.1947 morning, we along with 3 other families were allotted a room on the first floor. Most of the shops were owned by Hindus. When they came to know that many Hindu displaced families had been put up in the market, they came in the late morning and opened the shops and invited the Hindu families staying there to come and take anything they need free of cost. We brought dry fruits: almonds, pine nuts, walnuts, etc. Our mother asked our father to bring white cloth '*Than*' (50 yards roll) and needle and white thread. Open space of the market was still under water. In front of the shops was corridor. It was at slightly higher level from the level of water. There were 5–6 cloth shops. We entered the first shop and as pre-decided, we picked up one '*than*' of white cloth. It was quite heavy. Our father took it alone. We both the brothers started search for a shop of needles, thread, draw string and buttons for shirts and a scissors. We made another trip to the market to bring *atta*, jaggery, sugar and ghee and a few kitchen wares.

First thing first, our mother and both sisters – elder one Bhiranwan and the youngest one Sheela started stitching dresses for all of us. Under wears were the first to be stitched one for each. Next was 2–3 dresses for the kid – Kishori Lal and 4 spread sheets. The owners' association of the market had made arrangements for lunch and dinner at the community kitchen (*Langar*). All the ladies of all the 4 families slept in the room and men and boys slept in the corridors.

4.9.1947 was a new day, a day of city life, similar to the days we had spent in Lyallpur in January 1946. Our mother got up early as usual. She was through of her morning routine and after 20 days she was performing *pooja.* The *prasad* was made from the jaggery, we had brought the previous day. It was made keeping in mind the number of people present there. Everybody who ate the *prasad* felt some sort of solace at heart. In those testing and troubled times performing *pooja* and arranging the *prasad* was unthinkable. The elderly persons blessed her pious act of unshakable faith and trust in God.

Our mother and the sisters picked up the work from where they left it off on the previous day. The day was fixed for stitching dresses at least one for each one of us. The ladies from the other 3 families offered their support. The work was divided. Our mother cut the cloth for 4 salwars. The size of each salwar was different. However, the salwars for both of us (brothers) was kept the same. Our father was not using salwar. A *Dhoti* was made for him. She noticed all the 3 ladies were good in stitching. She cut one salwar for herself also. By the time it was lunch time much of the stitching work was completed.

On way to take community meal (*Langar*), our mother suggested the ladies that they should make at least some spread sheets. The ladies talked to the male members of their families about the suggestion our mother had made. They brought cloth of their choice. Our mother suggested them to make their own spread sheets. And in the meantime she cut the cloth for shirts – one shirt for each one of us. Fold on the top of the salwars was done by our mother with some specific purpose. The draw strings were inserted in the presence of all of us. The salwars were ready to use and tested for the size of each one of us. The ladies took some rest and we boys went out to play. In the evening there was still bright light. In that part of the country the sunset was late. The ladies were again at work. It appeared that all the 4 families in the room were members of a one big joint family. Sleeping arrangement was the same, ladies in the room and gents in the corridors.

5.9.1947 was also a bright sunny day. After performing their morning rituals, the ladies again picked up the work they had left off the previous day. We, both the brothers, went out with strict instructions that we would remain together. Our mother advised us to bring cloth for making *dupattas* (kind of a scarf). At the cloth shop we spotted white cloth normally used for *dupatta*. We picked it up and from the adjoining shop we took some more dry fruit. We handed over all the pickups to our mother. The ladies were stitching shirts. It took more time to stitch a shirt. Since they had no other job to do, they were at it. They were from the same vicinity, they knew some of the relatives of each other. They had started gossiping. They felt relaxed and relieved of the pressure experienced during the last 20 days.

In the afternoon we were told that we would be shifted to another camp near to the railway station. We should be ready to board the train as and when it would come for final journey to Hindustan. The army officer was a Hindu Gurkha. He assured us that from then onwards we were under their protection. The name of the next camp was Ram Lal-ka-Gud-ka-karkhana. He further announced that Gurkha regiment has already been posted around this camp. The train might take 2–3 days to reach Hindustan.

Our mother told the other ladies that all of us should prepare for our onward journey. We should prepare something to eat during our journey days. They agreed. Our mother sent us to bring some more *atta* and *ghee*. The ladies went to the persons organizing the community kitchen and requested them to allow them to cook *Mann* to be used during the journey days. *Mann* is a form of *roti* – thick but smaller in size. *Mann* was stuffed with dry fruits and jaggery. The second type was in sugar. And the third one with salt and other spices. Four packets were made to be carried one by each one of us. It could be used in any time and it would not decay in the next 3 months. The persons managing the community kitchen suggested to the other families in the camp, if they wanted, they could also cook *Mann* to carry with them during the train journey. The other three families felt happy to carry something to eat during the train journey. The ladies were back on their job to complete stitching of shirts before the sunset. *Dupatta* – one each for a female person in the family was stitched.

The evening of September 5, 1947 brought a big relief and some smile on the faces of all of us. The vested interests (terrorists) came to know that the owners have kept open the shops for the refugees. In the evening once again we heard the shouting of Allah-hu-Akbar. The smile we had a little while ago vanished instantly. Without wasting any time the Gurkha regiment personnel made an announcement on the loud speaker that they were taking care of those mis-adventurous persons. We should not get panicky. We went to take our meals/dinner fearlessly. Before we could go to sleep, it started raining. It rained cats and dogs. The corridors had become wet. We had to sit for some time till the water got dried up. One gentleman started cutting jokes. It made us laugh and the hushed laugh could be heard from inside the room. Our father narrated the horrifying situations we had undergone and how we were hounded by the terrorists. The only redeeming factor was that there was no casualty in our family.

September 6, 1947 morning we all were excited that we would be finally moving to a camp where our ordeals would end. We would soon enter our new homeland – Hindustan. The Indian army trucks came around 9 a.m. We were desperately waiting for the army personnel to announce to proceed to the next camp. All of us rushed towards the trucks with whatever belongings we had. Other families, it appeared, had not been uprooted as we were. Each member of the family was carrying 1 trunk/steel suit case. The boxes seemed to be containing some clothes and valuables. Possibly, that was the reason the other 3 ladies did not show any interest in stitching clothes for themselves.

Seeing the mob, the army personnel became alert. They suggested we should not panic. They advised us to stay at some distance. They called 5 men standing in front of the mob. They suggested that all the family members of those 5 men should come forward. The army official confirmed from those 5 men whether all their family members had come. They noted the name of male member of the family and the total number of members in the family. The other army official advised the waiting people that they should gather their family members in a similar way. That would help them and us (the refugees) to board the truck comfortably. The army officials allowed only the required number of families as per their norms. They assured the families remaining that they would bring back the trucks and take them in the next trip. The camp was not at a far off distance.

In just 10 minutes we were at Ram Lal-ka-Gud-ka-karkhana. The camp was very close to the railway line. In the next trip the remaining people were brought. We all the 4 families were united once again. Before leaving our father had gone to thank the members of market for the care, concern, help and the trouble they had taken for all of us. During the discussion, the market men had told him (our father) that they had already sent their families to Hindustan in the first train and they all were fine. The train we would be boarding would be the seventh. They had further informed him they would come by air, only after ensuring that no one was left out in the Jhang Mandi camp.

Yet another wait started. The ladies were in their known groups they had made at Jhang mandi. The men were also idle. Our father struck an idea. He went back to the market in the army truck. He enquired from the market association members if they had a chess board and playing cards. They were kind enough to provide chess board and playing cards. He returned in the same army truck. He handed over 4 packs of cards to the men sitting idle. For those who were not farmers it was a normal time pass in their respective places. Our father found a chess player. Soon there were many advisers to them. One of the army personnel had seen them playing chess. He was fond of the game of chess. In the afternoon he was relieved of his duty. He came and told them that he would come to join them after changing his dress/uniform. The army men in white and black continued their battle.

Then the real army man came. He was given the choice of selecting the pieces white or black. He picked up white pieces. He was a good chess player. He was not used to have so many advisers around. He being a chess player had lot of patience and did not react to the advice of on-lookers. In any case everybody enjoyed the game. The card players had also been entertaining themselves.

For some time our mother was alone. She cut 4 pieces of cloth slightly wider than the width of a 100 rupee note. In three cloth pieces she rolled 2 notes of Rs. 100/- each and in the 4th only 1 note was inserted. Both ends of each cloth were stitched in such a manner that draw string could pass and move freely. One each folded cloth containing 2 notes of Rs. 100/- was pushed along with draw string in to the waist fold of salwar of my mother, elder sister and my elder brother. The remaining one folded cloth containing 1 note was inserted along with the draw string in my salwar. The day at the camp seemed to be very long, especially, for the ladies to pass. They had no work to do. They were not used to sit idle.

They decided to go to take lunch at the community kitchen. The protection assurance given by the Gurkha regiment made them care free. The ladies told them (men folks) that they were going for lunch, the men responded unmindfully. The ladies, on their return from taking lunch again reminded them to go to take their lunch. The Gurkha army officer who showed interest to play with them and had gone to change his uniform, they went to take their lunch.

The Gurkha army officer on his return found that there was nobody. It was not a surprise for him recalling that they had gone for lunch. Seeing him standing all alone one of the elderly lady asked "brother did you have your lunch? If not, go join them, they have gone to take their lunch". The army officer politely expressed that he had his lunch after he was relieved of his day's duty. And responded, thanks sister for showing concern about my welfare. She continued the discussion with the officer on various aspects. Her son had sacrificed his life in the World War II. She had known about the hardships the personnel in the army had to undergo. The lady and the army officer became emotionally charged. The army Gurkha officer had left his family behind a couple of years ago. What made the army officer surprised was that even in such trying conditions, we were behaving like a big family.

The menfolk returned after taking lunch. A gentleman from behind remarked, "Officer a mother would always be a mother. Officer come let us command our armies on the chess board". The army officer behaved as a member of a large family. The day passed fearlessly without much stress. Around sunset some terrorists tried to raid Jhang market. The Gurkha regiment personnel were there to protect the market from those terrorists. Shouting of Allah–hu-Akbar could be heard by us at Gud-ka-karkhana. Noticing so many army personnel near the market the terrorists went back.

September 7, 1947

People in the Gud-ka-karkhana camp appeared to be much relieved. The Gurkha army officer had indicated that a train might come on that day. In the evening, around sunset the train arrived. It was a goods train. To accommodate more number of persons some additional compartments were attached. People were in a hurry to board the train. The army personnel came and advised us to keep at a distance. Those who had already boarded the train were asked to check if any of their family members had been left behind and only those persons were asked to board the train.

The army personnel announced that we were to stand in a queue and ensure that all the family members were together. The Gurkha regiment officials tried their best that the compartments were not over crowded. All of us were in hurry to board the train and leave Pakistan. Unfortunately for us we got an open compartment. Many persons entered the train by climbing the compartment from the sideways. The compartment was so much over crowded that we could not stretch our legs. There were Gurkha guards to protect the train from miscreants. It was completely dark.

That same evening the train moved. We heard different slogans from different compartments: *Har-Har Mahadev, Jai Mata Di, Jo Bole So Nihal – Satsriakal.* Many people started praying. Praying for safe journey to our new homeland. It being a goods train had more compartments and some additional compartments were attached to accommodate more number of people. The speed of the train was limited. It was a cloudy dark night. Taking advantage of the darkness some terrorists tried to sabotage, harm the people, and steal things they could lay hands on. They could not succeed. The Gurkha regiment guards were alert. They fired in the air. Those who were trying to board the train jumped and ran away. We kept hearing the slogans Alla-Hu-Akbar.

September 8, 1947

Before the dawn, we had crossed Lyallpur (Now Faisalabad). The train had not touched the platform. It, being a goods train, was allowed to pass from the last track. As the sun rose, the day was bright. We again started hearing the shouts of slogans. The train stopped. The Gurkha army guards came and told every compartment that the train would halt for an hour. "For your natural calls you could make use of the nearby fields and in case there was anything alarming, please shout whereever you are, we (army personnel) will come immediately. We should not pay any heed to the slogans. The train would start after 1 hour. We would ask the train driver to give first whistle 10 minutes before the train would start."

After getting free from our natural calls many persons stretched their legs by lying on the grass. The train over stayed. As the compartments were over crowded people could not sleep. Now they could get a nap. People were feeling much relaxed. There was a well nearby. Many persons took bath and got refreshed. The other 3 families, we stayed together at Jhang Mandi and Gud-ka-karkhana had boarded the train's covered compartment.

We all ate *Mann* in the morning as a breakfast. The problem was that there was no milk for the kid Kishori. We noticed an army Jeep followed by a truck were coming towards our train. The Gurkha army guard was alert. He challenged the jeep nearing the train. He got response from the personnel in the Jeep. They had brought milk for the children up to the age of 2 years. Vessels containing hot milk were loaded in the guard cabin. They carried 1 vessel for 4 compartments. Milk was distributed in their presence. Some parents did not have utensil to take milk. The army officials had visualized it. They had brought earthen pot to serve and feed the kids. People in the train were overwhelmed for that thoughtful gesture to feed the kids and blessed the army officials for that thoughtful act. The mothers assuming that if milk was not available in the evening, they kept some milk for the evening. The army officials went back. We came to know that the Gurkha army guards had requested on wireless the army personnel at Lyallpur refugee camp to arrange milk for small kids. That was the reason the train was over delayed by an hour. The train moved on its onward journey.

Covering a good distance the train again stopped. The persons who had been travelling to Lahore noticed the train was not going to Lahore. They were right, the train was going to Shekhpura. The train was stopped at quite a big distance from Shekhpura. Everybody started guess work why train had stopped. There was no answer. The train stayed there for the whole night. The doors of the closed compartments were kept open, so that cool breeze could give some comfort to the persons sitting inside.

Our compartment being open one, it was over crowed, we could hardly sit comfortably. In the early morning of September 9, 1947 ladies were allowed to go for their morning calls in the nearby fields. Our Gurkha guards stood alert. The men were carefree. They came down, tried to relax. It was a double line. In case another train would come from the opposite direction it would pass without any obstruction. The men lied down on the sides of the track. Some of them had some sleep, because they were unable to sleep in the compartment. As the sun came up most of them moved under the shade of nearby trees. Some of them had sound sleep. This time problem was two fold – no milk for the kids and no drinking water for anybody. The ladies of the open compartments were the worst affected by the scorching sunshine. They were unable to get down from the train as the track was on much higher level. Some young ladies did venture to come out of the train and sat under the shade of trees. Thankfully our mother thought of carrying *Mann*. It saved us going hungry. We used *Mann* cautiously.

The men dared to go beyond the fields in search of a well to arrange drinking water. The guards allowed them to go with instructions that if they sense problem they would raise alarm by shouting loudly. They did find a well. They quenched their thirst. Many of them came running to take utensil to bring water for their family members. The army guards suggested that they could fill empty pots lying in the train's guard cabin. In case of some emergency that drinking water would be used.

On 9.9.1947 evening Gurkha regiment personnel made milk arrangements for small kids and dinner for others. It was a very big relief for all of us, as we had not eaten for the last

24 hours. After we had finished meals, a mob in large numbers again tried to attack the train. Their attack was foiled by the alert Gurkha army guards. The slogan shouting – Allah-hu-Akbar continued till mid night. It was horrifying night. Nobody could sleep. People in the train started praying. Their prayers too continued till mid night. We came to know that the root cause of those attacks on our train was a rumour that persons migrating from Hindustan to Pakistan by train were attacked, and thousands of Muslims migrating by that train were massacred. As a result, people from Shekhpura and the surrounding areas were retaliating.

The army guards tried to confirm about the rumour from the Gurkha regiment posted near the border. They were informed that no such thing had happened. How much a rumour can damage the sentiment of people! They were later on reassured that nobody would come even near the train. That was a concern for the army personnel – to protect people migrating from both the sides.

On 10.9.1947, around 10:00 am finally the train moved towards Lahore. Here again the train was diverted to the last track. It did not touch main platform of Lahore. As the train was nearing the border, people again started praying that the remaining short distance could be covered safely.

On 10.9.1947 afternoon the train entered finally in our new homeland – Hindustan. The atmosphere was rented by our Slogan: *Jo Bole so Nihal Satsriakal, Bharat Mata di Jai, Har Har Mahadev,* etc. The train stopped at Atari railway station. We were given at Atari a grand welcome. Compartments' gates were opened. Elderly persons were garlanded. A sardar saheb came and addressed us saying:

> *"Behno te bhravo, tuhada Bharat desh vich swagat hai.*
>
> *"Sab ton pehlan vaheguruji da prashad khao"*

"Pakistan vich jo hoya uss te mitti pao"
"Naan ley ke age vadh jao"
"Ghabraon di koi lod nahin"
"Vaheguruji sab bhaala karan ge"

Volunteers brought *Pattals* (plates made of leaves) with full meal. After 3 days people could eat to their hearts' content. Around 8:00 p.m., we reached Amritsar railway station. The platform was decorated with flowers and lights. We all got down from the train. We were allowed to sleep at the platform.

New Homeland – *Bharatvarsh*

On 11.9.1947 we were residents of our New Home Land – *Bharatvarsh*. It was also a fact that we had no residence to live in. We were labeled by a new name 'Punjabi Refugees'.

As advised by a sardarji at Atari railway station, we remembered our God and started marching forward. We boarded the first available train to Jalandhar. The first refugee camp in Bharat for Punjabi refugees was in Government College, Jalandhar. It was a huge complex. For people like us coming from the remote small village, it was amazing. It had many class rooms of big height and size. Each room had big windows on two opposite walls. Wind coming through the windows was comforting us. All the rooms were connected with each other. Door side of the class rooms had corridors. Rooms and corridors were at a height 3 feet from the ground. The rain water did not enter the rooms. However, in the centre of the compound in between the rooms there was rain water logging at knee deep level.

Some chairs were floating in the water. It appeared as if somebody had thrown those chairs into the water. Some of us waded through the water and brought those chairs into the rooms. Men had no work to do. Women had no work to do. Only we children had everything to do – play, play and play!

The college had boundary walls. Hockey and football were the two outdoor games most commonly played in the Punjab. It appeared that both the games were played within the boundary walls. We decided to do some work. The work was in front of us. It was decided to drain out rain water accumulated in front of the corridors of the open compound. One of the inmates of the refugee camp was an Ayurvedic doctor. He was

happy, rather amazed to see people were aware of cleanliness and hygienic need of the time and had volunteered to take precaution against infectious diseases. He came and explained to the people what wonder children had done. "We had decided to leave the camp", said the doctor. "The single reason was water logging which could cause malaria. On seeing you all under taking jointly such a difficult task, we would remain here with you all. I am an Ayurvedic doctor. I would be too glad to render my services any time needed by any one of you".

After the rain water was drained out, the ladies took over the charge of cleaning the compound. It was completely cleaned by lunch time. Ladies first, they were asked to go and have their lunch at the community kitchen (*Langar*). The organizers of the community kitchen greeted and welcomed the ladies with folded hands. They had come to know about maintaining cleanliness in the college. They had prepared a special sweet dish for the inmates of the camp. Punjabi refugees who stayed prior to our coming in the camp had damaged many things of the college, commented one of the organizers. Nobody liked such a mischief.

Our elders were busy in making the camp worthy of living. We youngsters decided to go out of the camp to explore unknown areas. The roads were not so busy. A very few vehicles could be seen on the roads. Yes, Bi-cycles and *Tongas* could be seen in good numbers. We saw many persons were having blankets. One of the elder boys of our group enquired about those blankets. We were told that in a nearby village Sheikhavati, plenty of blankets are lying there and there was nobody to use those blankets. Many things normally used by army personnel were lying there.

We all decided to go to the village. It seemed the village was converted into a temporary cantonment. It was then lying deserted. Each one of us took one blanket each. My elder brother saw an overcoat. He picked it up for our father. Gradually, our baggage was becoming bigger. Our elders had a peaceful sound sleep after one month. On 11.9.1947 we felt, really, we were in Independent India – *Swatantra Bharat* (our new homeland) without any fear of getting hurt or hounded.

12.9.1947 was the day to reckon with in our new homeland. The period from 12.8.1947 evening to 10.9.1947 afternoon was a period of transition, a period of unforgettable miseries. It had become part of history of our life. The words of Sardar Saheb on the platform of Atari railway station were remembered once again. We all family members sat together and had sweet *Mann* as breakfast. Our father inspired us that the time had come to act on the advice of Sardar Saheb: "Forget the past and move forward, no looking back". We had to survive and we would survive. We had already defeated death.

My mother said we would not live on those *Langars* (community kitchens) anymore. We should make our own earnings for our livelihood. Every one of us would work. Any work we were capable of doing, we should take up. With that resolve, we both the brothers went to Shekhavati village. We had seen the previous day green chillies had grown to their full size. Both of us brought those green chillies. We sold those chillies. We earned some amount, gave it to our mother.

12.9.1947 was the day of great significance for both of us. We had made our first earning in our life. Before going to take dinner, immediately after the sun-set at the community kitchen, our mother advised us to go to the nearby temple. She gave us a 1 paisa coin to offer to the almighty God a part of our first earning. My father suggested that better we all go and pray that God should bless us to carve our destiny at the earliest. We also went to the adjoining Gurudwara and made similar prayer that evening itself. After prayers we took our dinner. We were happy and relaxed. Our mother appreciated our (both the brothers) courage and efforts of earnings at that age. She commented 'my both sons' would be capable of taking responsibility of the family.

On 13.9.1947 both of us went to Shekhavati again to bring green chillies. We sold those chillies directly to the ladies of a residential area. They paid the price we quoted. Sale proceeds were more than expected. In the meantime, our mother had discussed with our father as to which of the things were to be bought to cook our own meals on the morning of 13.9.1947. Our father bought all the items required for cooking. There was yet another item we had heard of for the first time. It was *Dalda* (vegetable oil). It resembled to pure ghee. The shopkeeper was inquisitive to know as why he (our father) was buying things in such small quantities. The items were sufficient for our two meals.

Our mother made a temporary *Chulha* (cooking stove) using bricks. Only left out item was fire-wood. Fire-wood stall was at a far distant place. We were not sure for how many days we would be allowed to stay in that camp, it was planned to buy the required item on the daily basis. The only alternative was to request the organizers of community kitchen to lend us some firewood which could be sufficient for 3–4 days cooking.

He had to narrate about our decision to be on our own. Our children have already started earning. The organizers of the camp were overwhelmed with joy to know that even in such difficult situations we were trying to keep our self-respect and wanted to be self-reliant. They assured that they would send the required firewood which could be used in small *chulha.* They had big and heavy pieces of firewood. They had further assured that any time we could approach them for any help. As assured they sent firewood after some time. Our decision and action became the topic of the camp. Many young volunteers came and sought blessings from our parents. We were appreciated for our contribution to the laudable achievement.

Next day on 14.9.1947 our father went to the same shop. The owner was a young man. He had also heard about our decision and action. With folded hands he bowed before our father as a mark of respect. He said that he had learnt, even in adverse situation, one should not surrender but face the situation courageously. Our father bought the required items for the 2 meals of the day. The young shop owner gave special discount and requested that till he (our father) was there in the camp, he should keep buying all the requirements from his shop. There was no problem of communication. The mode of dialect was the same in the Punjab. Our father tried to get job in some shops. He did not get the job. The reason was uncertainty as to how many days he would be in Jalandhar.

He went to wholesale market where casual workers were always in demand. He got a job at the wholesale grain merchant. He sold some bags of wheat. He calculated the value and asked the buyer to go and pay a specific amount to the owner. The buyer took money to hand it over to the owner. The calculation of amount was correct up to paisa. The owner was surprised to see that a casual worker was so much accurate in calculating the value of wheat sold. He was paid Rs. 2.00 for the day, as daily wages.

On 15.9.1947 he went to the market and enquired if there was any work for that day. Instantly the grain merchant asked him to do the job he did the previous day. He sold the grains. The owner was negotiating a deal with some other trader. Our father took a piece of paper noted the net weight and the value worked out for weight of grains. Asked the buyer to go and pay the amount to the owner. It was a bigger surprise for the trader to see accurately calculated and neatly written amount. The grain merchant could not resist his inquisitiveness and enquired who he was, because a casual worker to be so accurate, he had never seen in the past. Our father had to tell him all the facts, including that he himself was a business man. The trader paid double the amount for that day and asked him to come every day till he was in Jalandhar. On his return he asked us that there was no need for us to do the business, he had been assured of a job till we were in Jalandhar. The next 2 days, 16th and 17th September 1947 we were in Jalandhar camp.

On 18.9.1947 we had to leave the camp. We were asked to go to the Punjabi Refugee Camp at Ludhiana. We all went to the railway station. The train for Ludhiana was to leave after about 2 hours. Our father went to the merchant (market was not at a far of place) and expressed his gratitude for the support he had extended in the last a few days. The trader wished him the best of luck for the future. Our father returned well in time. The train had already come on the platform. In the evening we reached Ludhiana. The train journey was free of charge. At the platform we enquired the location of Punjabi Refugee camp. It was at a walking distance and we walked down to the camp.

There were many boys of our age in the camp. We boys in the evening went on chatting. We told them about our adventure at Jalandhar and Shekhavati. We both the brothers thought of exploring similar adventures in Ludhiana also. We talked to the other boys if they were ready for the adventure on the next day – 19.9.1947. The boys readily agreed and were excited to do some thing they had not done before. All of us went and talked to our parents about our plan for the next day. Once again we had to eat at the *Langar* (Community Kitchen) at Ludhiana.

On 19.9.1947 morning we boys got out of the camp. We took the first road leading to the fields. After walking about 2 miles we saw a village. We went to the village. It was completely deserted and damaged. We searched the whole village. Maize crop was ready to be reaped. Not a single soul could be seen there. In the surrounding fields, corn cob had grown to its full size. Both of us plucked 12 pieces each. We were finding it inconvenient to carry corn cobs. While we were roaming in the village my brother had noticed some net-like cloth in one of the houses. He brought 3 nets and made 2 bundles of those plucked pieces. We sold about 20 pieces near the railway station. The sales proceeds were not as expected. It was a hot day. We reached the camp in the afternoon. We were hungry. Our mother advised us that we should go and take lunch as the community kitchen might close soon. We did so. Both of us were tired. We slept till late evening. Our parents advised us not go to the village next day.

On 20.9.1947, our father had tried to get work in the market. He could not get it. We also did not venture to go to the village as advised by our parents. About sun-set we all boys assembled in the compound of the camp. We started playing *Kabaddi.* Many elderly persons came. In the Punjab State, *Kabaddi* had been most popular game. They hooted and shouted on every point irrespective of winning or losing. The period they had been witnessing the game they forgot what the traumatic conditions had been in the last 40 days. A gentleman became the self-appointed referee. His decision was accepted by all the players. Nobody even once questioned his authority as referee.

It appeared boys were very good players. It took more than an hour to finish 1 game. A group of ladies who were to take their dinner stopped and enjoyed the game. On completion of the game they announced "it was dinner time boys you need to eat well". It confirmed that a child was present in everybody, young or old, ladies or men. The day passed with relaxation.

21.9.1947. The day dawned. The sky was over-cast. There was a question mark "What do we do". Keep trying for a casual work, was one of the answers. Our father went to wholesale cloth market. Approached some shops and finally he got casual work. Father always used to wear a *Pagdi* (a head-wear). It had always been considered a status symbol and a mark of respect. A man without a *pagdi* did not get due respect. The style of tying and wearing *pagdi* enhanced a person's personality. It proved right. He was asked to attend to the customers. He welcomed the first customer of the day and modestly enquired about his requirements. The client was impressed. He was a regular client. He noticed the difference the way he was attended to and he used to be attended to in the past. The client met the owner negotiated the deals and placed the order. Before leaving he made a passing remark "The man seemed to be unlike a casual worker". They had no other client. The owner called my father and told him about the observations the client had made and expressed. The trader was a straight forward man. He repeated the words of the client, because of father paying attention to him (the client), he unknowingly had made extra purchases than the quantities he had planned originally to buy.

They were very much inquisitive to know every detail from our father. Our father felt uncomfortable to narrate the whole story. The trader reassured him that till the next client would come, they would like to hear from him. Most reluctantly our father told them, who he was, where from he had come and what he was. He further narrated the traumatic conditions he had been through during the past 40 days. "What the destiny had in store for us in the coming days, we did not know. We had no choice. We were accepting and facing all the situations smilingly. We were confident that we would succeed. The source of confidence, of optimism I got, was from my 2 young sons, 12 years and 10 years old. Both the boys took initiative to work and earned money at Jalandhar. They acted on the decision of their mother that we should earn for our livelihood. I worked at a grain merchant shop for 5 days at Jalandhar. That prompted me to search for work at Ludhiana as well". The cloth merchant too was impressed. He paid Rs. 5/- (Rs. 2/- towards casual wages and Rs. 3/- as commission for the extra business). The cloth merchant asked him to come to work for the days he (my father) would be in Ludhiana Refugee Camp. That incident was narrated by our father to all of us after we finished our dinner. It was a regular routine to sit together and express whatever we wanted to tell and whatever we had done in the day. We both were advised to enjoy with newly made friends.

22.9.1947 – The day was bright. The clouds played hide and seek. There were no rains for more than 2 weeks. The schools and colleges had not reopened. It looked second summer vacation. The boys made their respective age groups. Each group played the game suitable to their age. Even the girls also started playing. The ladies from the tents close to each other shared their thoughts. It appeared to be a family function. Men brought pack of cards. 4 persons played and 14 onlookers used to pass their remarks on every move. Worries of the ladies for their families could be seen on their faces. For the time they gossiped. They were really tension free.

On 23.9.1947, we were told to leave for Kurukshetra – our next refugee camp – by the late evening train. Yet another day of shifting. On his return from the market, our father got the news. We hurriedly finished our dinner. We left for the railway station. My father had already expressed his feeling that in case he (my father) would not come to the shop, it would mean that we were asked to leave by the late evening train to some other camp. We left from Ludhiana for our next destination – Kurukshetra.

24.9.1947 morning we reached Kurukshetra – the famous battle field of the Mahabharta. The camp was at quite a distance. We had no luggage. We walked down to the Camp. On the way, we saw a beautiful temple of the Lord Krishna. On the road, we also saw many army trucks coming and going. There was a big lake type pond. It was full of water. On 3 sides of pond, there were only army tents, away from the steps and banks of the pond. The 4th side, near the road, was kept open. It was meant for the devotees who considered it as 'holy water'. There were thousands of army personnel. It looked like a mini cantonment. About a mile away from the army camp, the punjabi refugees were allotted tents. The camp of army personnel and the camp of Punjabi refugees converted the small village of Kurukshetra into a big town.

On 24.9.1947 itself, a team of government officials came at site. They allotted tents to all the new comers-refugees. They recorded complete details about us in their record register. They gave us certain articles of our daily use: a mattress of the size of the tent, 2 blankets, 2 bedsheets, a broom, an empty tin for putting garbage or waste, etc. They further instructed us that winter season was going to set in. We would be staying in the camp for nearly 2 months. We could avail the following facilities, specially arranged by the government for all the refugees:

1. There was a dispensary. In case anybody in the family fell ill, we could go to the dispensary for treatment.
2. There was a ration shop. A specified quantity of ration would be issued from the ration shop for all the members of the family

3. You would be arranging cooking gadgets yourself as per your requirements.
4. For the next 7 days breakfast, lunch and dinner would be provided by the Government.
5. You could give message to your relatives, which will be announced on the All India Radio.
6. In case we wanted to go to meet our relatives, we could travel by train free of charge.

There would be no restriction. All of us or any one of us could go anywhere in India for any number of times.

After dinner we all sat together. We discussed about the next 2 months we were going to stay at Kurukshetra. It was not a big city where we would be able to get some work to earn for our livelihood. We could not get any answer. On 25.9.1947 morning, we again started thinking. Finally, our father said that he would go to Delhi in search of our cousins to seek their help and guidance. He did not have complete address. He only remembered that Mr. S.L. Dev was staying near Chandni Chowk opposite Lal Quila and was working in a medicine shop. My father could not locate him. He went back to the railway station. He stayed overnight at the railway station. Like him there were many persons searching their relatives.

A person sitting nearby had come in search of some of his family members. He was almost of his age. They started talking about the painful days they had passed. It was a sort of relief by exchanging their heart felt feelings. He had been in Delhi for the last 4 days. Any train that stopped at the platform, he would go to each compartment in search of his near and dear ones. The family members got separated at the time of boarding train. He belonged to Tehsil TOBA-TAKE-SINGH. They had developed a bond of some unexplainable relationship.

The unknown companion proved to be a great help. He took him (our father) to public announcement window. The window was opened specially for the convenience of ousted/ displaced persons from Pakistan. They registered his name and the message to be conveyed to the relatives. Within 5 minutes the first announcement was made. The announcer assured our father that if any response was received, it would be noted. That window would remain open for all the 24 hours. He could come and enquire any time.

On 26.9.1947, he checked with the announcer, there was no response. He went to the market in Chandni Chowk and Fatehpuri wholesale market. He purchased Sunlit soap and 50 packets of cigarettes. He returned to Kurukshetra by first available train. As anticipated he had not been able to locate Mr. S.L. Dev.

On 27.9.1947, all three of us were on our job to sell Sunlit soap and cigarettes at 2 different places. I was helping my elder brother. By lunch time we had sold a few packets of cigarettes and some cakes of Sunlit Soap. It encouraged us. In the afternoon heat of sunlight reduced. We were again on our business. By 28.9.1947 – in just 2 days all the packets of cigarettes were sold. The buyers were mainly army personnel. Sunlit Soap nearly half of the number, were left out to be sold. Next day 29.9.1947 our father went back to Delhi. On alighting from the train he straight away went to public announcement window. He enquired from the announcer if there was any response to the message he had left on 25.9.1947 night. There was none. He requested the announcer to keep announcing the message and he would come again after 4 days to enquire about the response.

He went to Fatehpuri market (in Delhi). He saw a shop of *paan-cigarettes.* Our father asked the shop-keeper about the wholesale market for cigarettes. Our father told him the truth about himself and purpose of coming to Delhi, when the *paanwala* repeatedly enquired. The *paanwala* offered him a cigarette. Our father politely expressed that he did not smoke cigarette. The shopkeeper was very much surprised to know that. He further enquired if he had eaten anything. The answer was in the negative. There was a restaurant across the road. He (the *paanwala*) asked our father to go to have rice *pullao*, the restaurant was famous for. Our father thanked him and requested him to help in giving the address of the cigarette dealer. The *paanwala* not only gave the address but gave him a note for some discount on his purchases. It appeared the *paanwala* had some relations with dealer. With the written note along with address, father went to meet the agent of a cigarette company. The note was written in Urdu. The cigarette dealer was big business man. He used to supply cigarettes in crates not loose packets. On seeing the note he (the dealer) instructed his man to give 50 packets each of three different brands and allow special discount normally given to a retailers. 150 packets of cigarettes were given to him in a jute hand bag.

He paid the amount and rushed to the railway station. He was able to catch the last train. He reached Kurukshetra in the night. By mid-night he reached the camp. We all had slept. Only our mother was awake. He was served dinner and then both of them slept. In his absence we had sold some cakes of soap and the remaining packets of cigarettes.

The army personnel were friendly. They frequently would come and enquire if they could be of any help. We boys were allowed to visit their units in the evening. Many a times they took us to their canteen. They would insist that we should sit with them and eat with them. It used to be a pleasure to eat with them. Some of us were non-vegetarians. All those boys would feel lucky to enjoy non-vegetarian food with those respectable persons. They would treat us as their family members. We learnt from them that there was a drink known as liquor (*Sharab*). Only the adults were permitted to drink. It was strictly prohibited for the children or even for grown up boys.

An army officer, Mr. Rao had developed some affection for us. He would come once in a while to call on us and enquire about our welfare. Our mother suggested to him since the winters were setting in, if he could bring some white wool she would like to knit for him a half sleeves pullover. He arranged white wool. As our mother and sister were free, it was knitted and given to him within a week. He was happy. He told us that he would be going out on a temporary duty and would be back after about a month.

During those days our youngest sister Sheela had fever. For two days she was treated with home remedies. There was no improvement. On the third day some red spots were noticed on her face. She was taken to the dispensary and it was diagnosed as chicken pox. There she was treated for chicken pox. She did not respond to that treatment. Our parents were advised that children should not be allowed to touch her. As a precautionary measure we, all three brothers, were treated with some medicine for chicken pox. Unfortunately, on the seventh day she breathed her last. Destiny hit us hard once again. A pious soul was snatched away from among us by the cruel hands of destiny.

The doctor along with his compounder visited each and every family in the camp to guide them that if they noticed anybody was sick they should contact them at the dispensary. The doctor later on told us that he had intimated about that case to the army hospital authorities and sought their help in the event of an emergency. Some days ago we had claimed we had defeated death, but destiny and death spare no body. We accepted it and reverted to our normal life with a heavy heart.

We took to our work. Certain army personnel enquired as to why we had not been coming to do our cigarettes business. Our father advised us that we could go and play. Near to our camp passed a railway line. We (our group of boys) crossed the railway line. We saw there was a dusty road and green fields as far as we could see. At the edge of the green fields there were creeper (leafy plants) having vegetables. Two of those vegetables we had never seen before, namely: *Parval* and *Karounda*. The third one – *Torri* we had eaten earlier often (it was a type of bottle gourd). All of us plucked some quantity of each of the three vegetables. Each of the vegetable made a very tasty dish. My elder brother went and relieved our father to take some rest. We children were enjoying gossiping and playing. At times some of us would quarrel on some trivial matters. The other boys would come and mediate and the matters patched up. All of us would start playing as if nothing had happened (forget and forgive would prevail). That is why we claim with pride that "we are childhood friends."

At some distance from the green fields we saw there was a large size hoarding containing painting of a chariot depicting Lord Krishna driving the chariot and Arjuna standing under the umbrella of the chariot. On the side of the chariot, there was a marble plate with an inscription in bold letters – G*ita Upadesh*. Alongside there was a small pond and a tall shady tree. People of Kurukshetra claimed it was the actual place where Lord Krishna guided the warrior Arjuna about what was right and what was wrong for a warrior on the battle field.

"This dialogue between the two was subsequently recognized as one of the most revered 'Holy epics – the *Bhagwat Gita*'." It is revered to the extent that in the Indian courts it represents the God. The complainants, defendants and the witnesses take oath keeping their hand on the Bhagwat Gita. They take the oath, "Whatever they would say they would speak the truth".

In the evening, after finishing our dinner we told the whole story to our family members. All the elders knew about the battle of Mahabharta. They were happily surprised but they did not show any interest to visit the place. We young boys continued exploring the nearby areas. One day we happened to land in a village called Thanesar. The villagers told us that their village was closely associated with the Mahabharta. The army fighting for the Pandvas stayed in their village. The days passed by. We again started going to the army camp. The *sentry* had known us and they would allow us to go inside. We were treated like family members. If we did not show up on a day, they would enquire about welfare of our families and as to why we did not come to the camp the previous day. We at that age had not understood why the special permission was extended to us (children). The possible explanation was – we were harmless small lovable kids. The army personnel were away from their families for some years. They could see in us their own children.

Thirteen days mourning period was completed. Certain rituals were performed. There was no need to go to Haridwar. Kurukshetra itself was a place where such rituals could be performed. We had overcome the grief partially. We resumed our routines – road side business of selling cigarettes. The remaining packets of cigarettes and Sunlit soap were sold.

Meeting the Sister

As the mourning period was over, our father could leave Kurukshetra. He went back to Delhi. He went to the public announcement window to find out if there was any response to his message he had left on 25.9.1947. Yes, a message response was there. In fact, they were worried why he did not contact

for so many days. The address of Mr. S.L. Dev was given. It was a walking distance from Delhi Railway Station. It was not difficult for him to locate the house, because he had treaded those lanes on his previous visits to search their house.

The long awaited search was over. He reached Mr. S.L. Dev's house. All, our *Bhuaji*, Mr. V.D. Dev with his wife and Mr. S.L. Dev and his wife, were anxiously awaiting his visit for the last many days. Meeting of elder sister and her younger brother was a touching moment. Other members of the family welcomed him affectionately. The immediate neighbor Mr. Gupta also came and expressed his happiness. First question our Bhuaji asked was about my elder Brother, Aienshilal. She had come to know from somebody that all the family members were together and safe but whereabouts of Aienshilal were not known, as when the riots took place, Aienshilal was in the hostel. It was followed by volley of questions.

Before he started narrating the whole traumatic story, Bhua Mehran took him inside the house and made him eat something. Both of them returned. Everybody was eager to know the details of the painful events and the stress and strain we had undergone during the last 2 months. They had read different versions of the atrocities inflicted on Hindus. Our father explained all the incidents right from 12.8.1947 to 10.9.1947 that took place in Pakistan and subsequently from 11.9.1947 onwards in Hindustan. It was so painful and pathetic that all the persons (men and women) sitting there had tears in their eyes. All the persons were so much affected with the incidents narrated by our father that they did not go to take their lunch. At the end our father repeated Sardar Saheb's inspiring words at Atari railway station:

Bheno te bhravo bharat wich tuhada swagat hai

Pakistan wich jo hoya uss the mitti pao

Waheguru ji da parshada chhko te agge vadh jao
Waheguru ji sab changa karan ge

"Those words we kept on telling ourselves. What was encouraging was that we all the family members were ardently acting in one voice on the advice of Sardar Saheb. Most satisfying was that our children did not succumb to the pressure of any eventuality. Rather they accepted and faced all the situations boldly in that age". Those words proved comforting to everybody present in the room.

It was late afternoon bhuaji said that everyone should take their lunch. Nobody realized that so many persons had gathered there and had not gone to their work. He stayed there for the night. He had met for first time Mrs. Sarla, wife of Mr. S.L. Dev. He felt sad that he could not give her the gift she deserved. She had heard so much about *Mamaji* (our father). She longed to meet us all. Dialogue between sister and brother was unending. After the dinner they reassembled in the backyard on the cots laid by the servant. Our father sought their suggestion as to what should be done next. Mr. V.D. Dev replied that we would be relocated in some bigger town. The farmers would be allotted land for farming in the villages. It would take some more months, and the process to allocate the district was in progress. Till the uncertainty for relocation prevailed we would have no option but to continue in the camps. For Jhang district displaced persons, the district for relocation would be in the Punjab State. Many refugees had not reached India. Around midnight other members of the family went to sleep. Sister and brother had so much to say and hear. They did not know when they were over powered by sleep. Next day morning, when they got up, both the brothers were ready to go to their respective offices. Our father told them that he would be going back to Kurukshetra the same day.

He took his breakfast. He was about to leave, when Sarla *bahu* brought and handed over a tiffin containing something to eat during the day. He went and met the *Paanwala* at Fatehpuri. Thanked him for his support on his last visit. He then said sorry for he had gone straight from cigarette shop to the railway station. He also told him about the untimely demise of his youngest daughter due to chicken pox. He said, he had to come because the following week would be Dussehra festival. So he would like to buy more quantities of cigarettes. The *Paanwala* again gave him a note addressed to the dealer of cigarettes. The dealer as usual was very busy due to Dussehra and Diwali festival bookings. Dealer's man recognized him. The man asked him to come to his counter. Our father purchased 600 packs, 200 packs of each brand. Our father told the man that he would be coming the following week to buy some more stocks for the festival season. The man assured him that he could come any time. He would be allowed the same discount. Like last time, he proceeded to the railway station.

There was enough time for the departure of the train. He went to 24 hours announcement window and thanked them for their help. He was able to meet his sister and her sons. He went back to Kurukshetra. We all were waiting for him, to know whether he was able to meet Bhuaji and other family members.

Our wait was over. His gleaming eyes and face conveyed that he had met everybody in Delhi. He was very much tired. All of us went to sleep. Our mother and sister had resumed the morning prayers. We finished our breakfast and went to work as cigarette vendors. It was opposite side of the army camp. People it seemed had missed those brands. They purchased one pack of each brand. We did brisk business that day. The following day again the army personnel purchased extra packets. We came to know that those who have made extra purchases were going on leave during the coming Dussehra and Diwali festivals to their native places. The same evening our father left for Delhi and brought additional stocks of cigarettes and *bidis*.

The Dussehra day came. Dussehra was celebrated in the army camp too. Our group of boys decided to go to the army camp. It was the day of *Bada Khana* (Special Meal). All ten of us were invited to have meal with them. All of us enjoyed the special meal. Some Army personnel used to have a stroll after meals. They came with us up to our camp. Parents of all of us were anxiously waiting for us. Seeing those army personnel with us, our parents felt relieved. It was a memorable evening.

Mr. Rao returned from his temporary duty. He came to see us. He felt sad to know about the untimely demise of our younger sister. He had also been sanctioned leave and was proceeding for his native place.

The days passed. In the army camp, special arrangements were being made for Diwali. It was 12.11.1947. They erected a small mountain – symbolizing the Himalayas. A Map of India was drawn on the walls of mini-Himalaya. On the borders small electric bulbs were fixed. In the middle of the map a painting of *Bharat Mata* holding a Trishul was drawn. On the north side was a Gurudwara, in the eastern side was the temple, in the western side was a mosque and in the southern side was a church. Those pictures were also decorated with electric bulbs. The crown of *Bharat Mata* was carved and studded with special type of marbles which had special effect of light, from the bulbs as if diamonds were twinkling. What we could not understand was the iron chains were falling from her neck, hands, body and ankles. As I grew up I came to know it depicted that during the British Rule she was enslaved with chains. Our people fought for her freedom. From 15th August 1947 onwards India got Independence and she was free from those chains.

Down below the knees was written:

Bharat mata ki jai. jai hind

We boys were specially invited to celebrate the Diwali. Some officers were also present on the occasion. An official made a speech. "Many Indians have laid their life to attain freedom. It is for us to keep it protected." He said, "We are the present. These youngsters are the future." They blessed us. Each one of us was given a packet of sweets. I vividly remember that picturesque scene of Bharat Mata even today after 65 years of first Diwali in Independent India, celebrated with the high officials of army.

We were dropped at our camp in their Jeep. We had informed our parents that we were invited at the celebrations of Diwali in the army camp. They should not worry about us, if we were late. It was inscribed on our mind because we never had any chance to witness such illuminations.

The winter season had already set in. We were used to such winters. The only difference was the blankets. While using the blankets we felt something was pricking. There was no alternative. After a week's time we were informed that we would be shifted to a new camp. The place of a new camp would be conveyed to us soon. Many thoughts started coming to our mind. We boys (friends) decided that we maintain our group. On 29.11.1947 we were conveyed that we were to go to new camp at Rohtak. It was a district place and a bigger city. On 1.12.1947 we reached Rohtak.

Life Goes on.....

On December 1, 1947 we reached Rohtak railway station. Pick up arrangements were made by the Government from railway station to Punjabi refugee camp. It was outside the city. The tents were of small size. Already there were many refugee families. Close to the refugee camp there was a beautiful public park. Certain parts of the park had shady trees. The same day the Government officials came and noted complete details about us:

1. Name of the head of the family
2. No. of family members
3. Age of each member
4. Name of the primary school where children were studying
5. Place of origin, we had come from.

They issued a card to us.

By showing that card we would be entitled to get ration for all the 6 members of the family on subsidized rates from the ration shop on daily/weekly or monthly basis as per our convenience.

In case of need we could get medical help from the Health Centre.

The children would get admission in school and in the same class they were studying in.

In the meantime, the district authorities had started using those parts of the park as *Bal Pathshala* (School) for the children of the refugees. The children were taught Hindi. The text book was provided by the school. The remote area of the Punjab state we had come from had not even heard about Hindi. There the medium of instruction was Urdu. The second language was English which was taught from 5th class in middle schools. The occupation of people in those remote areas was Farming. Majority of the students would drop out after primary education. Only a few boys would go and join middle school. The reasons for the drop out were:

1. Thinking of the parents – they were farmers. For a farmer's ward primary education was sufficient.
2. The student (boy) had to stay compulsorily in the hostel. The distance from the village to the middle school was too much. Commuting on day to day basis from village to school was strenuous.
3. Many farmers were not in a position to afford the additional expenses to be incurred for the stay of the boy in the hostel.
4. The benefits of education to the farmers needed to be explained and emphasized.

The next day 2.12.1947, we were admitted in the *Pathshala,* open to sky, under the trees. The teachers paid special attention to the refugee boys. We were excited to learn a new language. Our father met the teachers. He sought their advice about continuing our regular studies. They were happy to know the interest we had shown in continuing our studies. Syllabus was the same. Continuity of the course would be maintained.

They explained that for the time being there was no school nearby where the children could be admitted in their respective class. Secondly, it was uncertain for how many days, weeks or months we would be there in the camp. One of the teachers was kind. He suggested that we should buy Urdu text book and mathematics course book. He would teach us after Hindi class was over. We purchased the books as advised by him from the shop dealing in second hand books.

Our younger brother, Kishorilal, was over 1 year. He had started walking. We all family members would enjoy seeing him walk. He in return would greet us by his broad smile. After I used to return from *Pathshala,* he was my responsibility. We would play and our mother and sister would take him only when it was necessary. At times he would hold my finger and would make me walk with him. Whenever he wanted to express his anger, he would scream on us and draw our attention towards him. During the dark nights, we could play only up to sunset.

In a couple of days later our father went to Delhi. Rohtak was much nearer to Delhi. It took 3 hours by train to reach Delhi. Many of their other relatives, who had come from Pakistan and had stayed with Mr. S.L. Dev had left to settle down in Delhi. Our cousins were not aggressive persons. Two elder brothers who had come from Lyallpur as refugees also did not venture to occupy any house left behind by Muslim families, as they had left behind their house at Lyallpur. They had taken one room kitchen with common bath room on rent.

He (our father) met our Bhuaji (his elder sister Mehran). She was all alone in the house. He was surprised for not seeing any other person in the house. She told him about all the relatives. They were safe and together. The 1 BHK Apartment was too small to accommodate so many persons. They managed and adjusted between themselves happily.

He told her about our shifting to the new camp at Rohtak. Both of them talked about many aspects of hardship we had undergone. For survival, we had become cigarette vendors. He further told her about the sad demise of our younger sister Sheela. Both were emotionally charged and were in tears. He took his lunch. He took her permission to leave and go back to Rohtak. He went first to the cigarette dealer, purchased some cigarette packs and *bidi* bundles.

During those days the mode of local transport service was Trams in Delhi. The starting point was Chandni Chowk, opposite Lal Quilla to Fatehpuri-Khari Bawli. He travelled by tram to reach Khari-Bawli. Off Khari-Bawli was a big covered yard where those Trams were parked when not in use. From there he walked down to the cigarette dealer. He purchased cigarettes and *bidi* packs. On his way back to the railway station he came to Chandni Chowk *Ghanta Ghar* (Clock Tower), a huge tower. A big clock was fixed at the top of the tower. Inside the clock a bell was fixed. It would ring automatically on completion of an hour.

When he got down from the tram, the bell rang 4 times. That conveyed that it was 4:00 o'clock in the evening. He surveyed the markets in and around Chandni Chowk. For different trade, there was different market. There were no two-wheelers, auto-rickshaws. Goods into the market were delivered from main Chandni Chowk road by cycle-rickshaw or man pulled hand-cart. The markets were full of noise. One could hear different voice from different side to attract the customers. The approach roads to those markets were very narrow. Somehow, he was convinced cigarette selling on the road side was not the business he would like to continue. He made up his mind to come back to these markets to survey the way the business was done in those markets.

Nearby the *Ghanta Ghar* there was a big public park. Across the park was the railway station. At 5:00 p.m. there was a train for Rohtak. He boarded the train, reached Rohtak around 8:00 p.m. We were excited to tell him about our first day at the *Pathshala* (School). The *Pathshala* was specifically started for the children of the refugees. The boys of any age were enrolled to learn Hindi. He listened to our talks with full attention. In the process he did not get any chance to express his excitement he experienced in Delhi. It was only the next day night he narrated his experience of Delhi markets.

When he was narrating about the structure of the markets, I recalled that in January, 1946, I had noticed the similar structure in Lyallpur and Lahore, in August, 1947 at Government College campus and in the markets of Jalandhar and Ludhiyana, the infrastructure of all the commercial building had a corridor on the front side. The residential buildings were having 3-4 stories. On each floor there were small apartments. Each side of the stair case was a common bath room and lavatory on the ground floor. There existed such a facility was unknown to the small villages and towns.

On the second day, our Hindi teacher taught us the *Varnamala* (The alphabets of Hindi language. It comprised of 2 parts: 1) *Swar* (vowels) & 2) *Vyanjan* (consonants). He taught us to learn and understand both thoroughly. Since we were students of Urdu medium, he advised us to read those alphabets again and again. Those days the method of learning was to mug up by repeating it loudly. First 3 days he taught us only vowels. The method of repetition was applied here also. One student would stand up and read all the vowels, the remaining 24 would listen intently. Each student was required to read it turn by turn. At the end he would explain the position of the part of our mouth and the source of the sound viz-a-viz letters from the mouth.

Similarly for *Vaynjans* (consonants), he advised us to practice turn by turn for ten days. He allocated 10 days, because we were students of Urdu medium. He was not sure for how many days we would be in the refugee camp in Rohtak. The number of *Vyanjans* (consonants) was large. A group of the five *Vyanjans* originated from one source in the mouth. There were six such groups and for each group the source was different. The remaining 6 letters were combination of letters hence the source of these letters was also jointly from 2 parts of the mouth. On the seventh day itself he was convinced and happy that our batch had learnt to pronounce the letters well and fast. He guided us how and why these letters had been grouped based on the voice (phonetics). We moved on to the remaining part of the text book. We learnt the words also quickly. We found that not only our pronunciation was correct it was clear also.

We also started studying our regular course from the lessons we had left out at of the time of partition of the country from the teacher who promised to teach us after Hindi class. The partition had affected the studies of all the students for the period from middle of August – October, 1947. The teacher told us that due to the closure of the schools during the above period, we had not missed much of the syllabus. We would be able to cover up soon the studies we had missed.

Our taking to studies gave satisfaction to our parents. They never wanted we should drop out like the boys of the farmers. They were very much relieved on this aspect. The other aspect of life was sustenance. The business we had started as cigarettes vendor at Kurukshetra did not work well at Rohtak. People in Rohtak were more attracted to *bidis* smoking or *hookah.* We had to give up that source of income. One side there was no source of income and the other we were 6 members in the family to be fed. Since we had stared going to school, we were unable to contribute in any way to the sustenance of the family. Thankfully, the teacher, who was teaching us, did not charge any fee. The alternative source of income was thought of by our mother.

She knew the art of making certain circular seating thick mats (the like of circular mosquitoe coils). It was called *Moodha.* It was made out of *Sarkande* (One type of tall wild grass) and leaves of dates. And the *Chabbi* with covering lid (A type of today's casserole) for keeping *rotis* (chapatis). It made a colorful handicraft article. The third was storage drums made out of the same material with tight lids. These were of different sizes to store 25 kg. & 50 kg. Those drums used to be strong enough to hold the weight. The other use was to store quilts, bed sheets, pillows, mattresses and the dresses used for some special occasion. The material wild grass was freely available in the nearby green fields. The dates leaves could be purchased from the market. These leaves' original color had been off- white. These leaves could be dyed in any dark color. The stitching was done with those leaves only. The finished articles appeared very pretty and appealed to the eyes instantly.

It was winter season. It proved to be of great help to our mother and sister. After our brother was fed well, one of them would try to make him sleep in the sun. Winter sun shine was very pleasant. He would sleep for about 2–3 hours. Both of them would pick up their respective work of making artistic/ handicraft items.

The same day our father went to the nearby fields and brought the grass. The next day he went and purchased the dates leaves. My elder sister was a great help to our mother. Our mother taught her how to dye those leaves in different colors. The work was divided. Sister would dye the leaves and mother would stitch the mats and *chabbis*. For the first week the work was done without anybody noticing it. Most of the refugees in the camp were from the same remote areas of the district Jhang. Many ladies knew that art. Survival was a big question for all the inmates of the camp. Whatever both of them could produce was sold the next day. It was a novelty for the local people (in Rohtak).

It could not be kept a secret for long, as the dyed leaves were to be dried in the open. Care was taken that the dyed leaves were not exposed directly to sun light. After some days it became an open secret. Many ladies started making it. The shop-keeper from whom they purchased the date leaves started buying all the stocks the ladies could produce in the day. Our father was a business man. He negotiated with the shopkeeper to pay a part of the profit. The shopkeeper readily agreed with a condition that he (our father) would collect all the finished material and deliver at his shop and it would not be sold to any other trader. Secondly, the raw material they would continue to buy from him. We had found the means of our survival and also the survival of some other families who took to producing the articles of handicraft.

However, the income from those items was inadequate to maintain for the survival of 6 members in a family. We took to selling *Revadi* (one kind of sweet with a coating of white sesame seeds). Rohtak was famous for producing it. It was manufactured during winter season. It has been a common man's sweet. It is manufactured specially around Lohri festival (14th January). It was prepared in different varieties and sizes. Quality was the main variant in fixing the price. Better the quality, better the price.

From then on the days passed smoothly and the year 1947 came to an end without any further blood sheds. We were in our new homeland, waiting to find a home. We both the brothers had made good progress in our studies. We did not have any information about the whereabouts of our cousins, Mr. Ganesh Das and Mr. Nathuram, either at Kurukshtra or at Rohtak camps.

We entered the year 1948 with hope to have our own home soon. Our hopes seemed to be fulfilled. We were informed that we would be relocated at Jhajjar town, a tehsil of district Rohtak having a population of over 20,000 persons. Unfortunately, Jhajjar had not been connected by train. It was at a distance of around 45–50 Km. from Rohtak. It remained under developed city due to inaccessibility from big cities and no connectivity by train. In and around Jhajjar town the underground water level was deep and water was hard/saline. It could not be used as drinking water or for cooking. We got that feedback before we shifted to Jhajjar.

In the last week of January, 1948 our father and elder brother went to Jhajjar. They were happy to know that our Bhua Parvati's family and Bhua Mehran's daughter's family had already reached Jhajjar. Many families from Rampur and surrounding villages were also there. They decided to settle-down at Jhajjar. They stayed with Bhua Parvati, and started search for a house. They succeeded in finding a spacious house. The house belonged to Tehsildar of Jhajjar. Under tehsil Jhajjar there were more than 160 villages.

The evacuated properties of the Muslims who opted to go to Pakistan were sealed by the municipal committee of Jhajjar with all the house hold goods left behind by the evacuees. A refugee family that had migrated from Pakistan had broken the seal and entered the house without any permission. The family made a fortune. In the meantime they occupied a house in a similar way in Delhi. They decided to shift to Delhi. They were looking for a buyer to buy heavy house hold goods. Father and brother met them and negotiated the price of all the house hold goods they intended to sell with a condition that before they depart for Delhi, they would allow us to stay in the house. It was accepted by them. My father, elder Brother and two daughters of Bhua Parvati came and stayed for the night. The other family left for Delhi in the early morning of the next day. It was January 29, 1948. On 30.1.1948 the girls cleaned the house.

Finally, Choudhary Chelaram found a home for the family to settle down in our new homeland – *Bharatvarsh*. Subsequently, we got that house on monthly rental basis in our father's name from the municipal committee, Jhajjar. They decided to call us on 31.1.1948 from Rohtak.

Unfortunately, on 30.1.1948 evening Bapu (The Father of the Nation) Mahatma Gandhi was shot dead. Nobody had ever dreamt that the Father of the Nation would meet such a tragic end. There was unrest. All the big cities were put on alert. On All India Radio people were requested to pray to the almighty God that his departed soul rest in peace. January 31, 1948 was declared holiday. Our *Pathshala* was also closed. I came back from the school and found one of our relatives had come from Jhajjar to take us to Jhajjar. There was nothing much to be carried by way of luggage. Only a few daily use articles were packed in a gunny bag. Before noon we travelled by bus. It took about 1½ hours and we were at Jhajjar. The house was at a walking distance from bus stand. The life at refugee camps came to an end. We were all happy that we got a house with all facilities in a much bigger city. The kid Kishori Lal got lot of space to move around. We were relieved of tension of his going out of the house.

Without wasting any time, we were admitted to the classes, we were studying at the time of partition. Accordingly, I was admitted in 4th class in primary school and my elder brother in 6th Class in middle school at Jhajjar. The annual examinations as usual took place in the month of March 1948. We were promoted to the next class.

I was also admitted in the middle school. The school was not at a far of distance. We could walk playfully. In middle school the monthly fee was 1 *anna*. The school was for both middle and high school i.e. from 5th to 10th Class. There were many class rooms. With resettlement of refugees in Jhajjar the number of students in each class had increased. It necessitated increase in the number of sections as well. The hostel was also attached to the school premises.